Personality of Tribal and Non-Tribal School Children

Ranjit Prasad Singh
PROFESSOR IN PSYCHOLOGY
T.M. BHAGALPUR UNIVERSITY
BHAGALPUR (BIHAR)

1998

DISCOVERY PUBLISHING HOUSE
NEW DELHI—110 002

Published by :

Discovery Publishing House
4831/24, Ansari Road, Prahlad Street
Darya Ganj, New Delhi—110 002 (INDIA)
Phone : 327 92 45
Fax : 91–11–3253475

First Published—1998

ISBN 81–7141–417–6

Laser Typeset by :

Allied Computers,
Karnal (Haryana)

Printed at :
Tarun Offset

Acknowledgement

I express my deep sense of gratitude to my friend and guide Dr. V.N. Singh, Head, Deptt. of Psychology, Marwari College, Bhagalpur for his valuable supervision during all phases of the study.

I owe a very special debt to my respected teacher Dr. U.P. Singh, University Professor and Head, University Deptt. of Psychology, Bhagalpur Univeristy, Bhagalpur for his comments, encouragement and help in more way than one, without which it would have been exceedingly difficult to complete the work.

I am thankful to Dr. R.C. Singh, Principal, R.D. College Sheikpura, Munger for his keen interest, encouragement and valuable suggestions.

I wish to acknowledge a special debt of gratitude to my respected father and also to Dr. (Mrs.) Usha Rani Singh, University Prof. University Department of Psychology, Bhagalpur University, Bhagalpur for their prudent guidance, co-operation and valuable suggestions.

I am also thankful to the tribal students and non-tribal students for their participation in the study. I also render my hearty gratitude to the teachers of Chandwa, Gumla, Lohardagga and Ranchi Schools for their co-operation made during data collection.

Lastly I must thank Sri Y.P. Jha, Typist, B.A.C. Sabour who typed the manuscript with great personal care and interest.

Ranjit Prasad Singh

Preface

Independence had a powerful impact in moulding the social, economic, educational and cultural life of the tribals. By and large the tribals are industrious, hardy, peaceful and simple-minded people and have to be admired for the uniqueness of their culture. However, they remain isolated from the main stream of national life and not only suffer from fatality of isolation but have also been victims of socio-economic discrimination and exploitation.

The socio-economic, educational and political development after independence have provided a new impetus to the forces of dynamism in the tribal India. Slow, but unmistakable changes are discernible among the tribals. Contact with urban people, spread of education, rising aspirations of the tribal youth, growth of social and political leaders all have combined to give rise to, what we may call, tribal elites.

Tribal students are the elite of their community. Naturally they will decisively shape the future of their community and its relationship with other communities. Unfortunately, not much effort has been made to understand them psychologically. This study is an attempt in that direction.

The psychology of personality deals with various problems concerning the development of personality. It is found that some students are good in their studies, while others inspite of their hard labour do not do well in their studies and are frustrated. This has led psychologists as well as researchers to investigate into the different dimensions of personality.

Till recently it was thought that intelligence was the only factor which brought differences in the educational achievement of students.

But many studies have shown that many non-intellectual factors, such as family background, personality structure, social factors, cultural factors, heredity, etc. are also responsible for the students' achievement.

The proposed research is an attempt to investigate certain personality characteristics of the school boys of two different cultures, tribal and non-tribal living and studying in villages and towns. The tribal personality is not claimed albeit, has been analysed in its entirety. Endeavour has been made in this study to investigage some personality factors (fourteen dimensions of personality) anxiety and adjustment (social, emotional, educational) of tribal students and to compare them with those of the non-tribal students. It is hoped that this study will help in understanding of personality characteristics of tribals in comparison to non-tribals.

Ranjit Prasad Singh

Contents

1
Introduction

Personality is an empirical field in the subject of Psychology. Many pioneer studies have been carried out in this field and on the basis of their findings many empirical laws have been formulated. Any study of personality involves the description and explanation of individual human behaviour in terms of certain general and relatively fixed responses that characterize the individual. In addition to the description of the individual, the psychological study of personality involves a theoretical and experimental attempt to explain the given personality formatives in terms of the dynamics of individual adjustments to various intra-and inter-individual events.

A human being does not grow up in a vaccum: his development is determined not only by the physical environment as the biologists proved, and by the family environment as Fraud (1936) demonstrated, but, as the massive data collected by the cultural anthropologists showed, by the larger societal and cultural institutions that are extolled, preached, and practised not only by parent "carriers" but by the leading minority (authority figures), if not by the majority, of the group in which the individual is reared (Kluckhohn & Murray 1953).

It is an established psychological truth now that a man in many respects is like no other man. Every individual's mode of perceiving, feeling and behaving has a characteristic pattern which is not precisely duplicated by that of any other individual. In short every individual's personality pattern—his temperament, intellectual abilities, adjustment, anxiety, self-esteem, aspirations and interests—differ widely from others.

The reasons behind the differences in the personality pattern of individuals may be seen both in the hereditary potentials and environmental conditions. Man begins his life as a biological organism. He receives some hereditary potentials from his forefathers on which he has no control. The remaining factors are environmental which vary from individual to individual and can be controlled and studied. Environmental conditions actually incorporate the influence of family, social-class and cultural factors on the growth and development of personality.

Individuals differ from one another with respect to the familial and social-cultural conditions in which they grow and develop. For example, their home conditions, socio-cultural conditions, anxiety, economic status, adjustment, physical and social environment may vary to a great extent, and the totality of these conditions influences the personality development. The socio-cultural conditions in totality may be favourable and unfavourable ranging from very favourable to very unfavourable.

In every society we find families with higher educational and occupational status and with sound economic conditions. In these families children are provided with satisfactory models to emulate and to identify with. But on the other hand we also find may such families which have various sorts of deprivations—economic, cultural, social, psychological and political. Lack of stimulating conditions, in such families do a great harm in developing the desirable traits in the children belonging to these communities. The members of these deprived social classes are called unprivileged or disadvantaged individuals. To the contrary, those individuals belonging to the upper class or privileged class are called advantaged individuals. The socio-class influences the personality in three ways—

1. It encourages or stunts the maturation of hereditary potentials.
2. It provides favourable or unfavourable personality pattern model for the children to identify with.
3. It either provides or denies the needed learning opportunities.

Through maturation, the hereditary potentials established at the time of conception eventually develop. Maturation, however, depends upon the environment and as such the hereditary potential will develop or will be hampered to the maximum depending upon the kind of environment, available to an individual, that is, upon the kind of social class in which the individual grows and lives. Good physical health on the part of the mother are favourable to parental environment and the normal maturation of hereditary potentials. The health of the mother influences the quality of nutritive substances, water and oxygen transmitted through the placenta to foetus (Montagu, 1962; Sontag, 1966). Maturation of hereditary potentials is generally slowed or halted for a short time after birth. If the birth is normal, the interruption in maturation will last only a week or so. If the birth is difficult or if during the parturition the brain or some other area of the body is injured, the halt will be longer (Miller et at., 1966).

Thus the disadvantageous environment has severe effect on the child development. A poor mother belonging to lower socio-economic status certainly lacks the advantageous environment and thereby produces a baby prone to many irregularities which are further aggravate by the impoverished dwellings in which the baby will grow and march the long way to maturation.

The second important way in which the socio-class conditions influence the moulding of the personality is by providing models for the individual to follow. A model means the ideal figure that incorporates in general the traditions, values, norms, codes and standards of particular cultural or sub-cultural group. A model that is acceptable to members of the group with the person is identified acts as a guide for him as well as for those who are responsible for training him to conform to social expectations.

There is a wide variation in modelling pattern of different cultures. In the Soviet-union, for example, there are strong social pressures to shape each child into the pattern of the "ideal person" whose service is dedicated to the state rather than to individual gains. The American concept of "ideal person" is different. In America the ideal person is one who puts high value on such qualities as personal output of energy, ability to adjust, mobility, optimism, competitiveness, honesty, prestige, anxiety and so on (Gillian, 1955).

Similarly, every culture has its modelling pattern which decides what kind of personality pattern it wants in its members and then sets up norms of approved behaviours. How does the culture modelling pattern decides the course of personality development has been described by Allport (1961) in the following manner:

a. The cultural tradition determines the lessons the parent will teach the child and the way in which the lessons are taught.
b. That different cultures have different ways of training the child and different lessons to teach.
c. That the child's early experience exerts a lasting effect upon his personality.
d. That similar experiences will tend to produce similar personalities within the culture.

We also find sub-groups in the same cultural group and consequently variations in the modelling pattern. This is why we find individuals of two subcultural groups of the same culture differ in their personality patterns. For example, in India we have different subcultural groups. They share the common Indian adjustment anxieties and values but there are differences in the degree of emphasis they put on particular value system. Differences among sub-cultural groups are due to the differences in the methods and techniques employed in the training of their neonates. This is the third important way that the personality pattern is moulded differently in different social classes. In this connection it should be remembered that there are two types of learning techniques. One is inner-directed; that we may call "identification", and another is outer-directed; that we call "child-rearing" in which outer agencies like parents, teachers and significant people come in contact with the child and influence his maturation and growth.

It is due to identification of a child with his parents that he adopts either desirable or undesirable characteristics which his parent embody. However, there is no perfect agreement between the characteristics of the child's personality and those of his parent's (Haris, 1958). This is due to other factors which operate simultaneously with the modelling pattern.

Thus we see that different socio-cultural groups differ in their modelling pattern and child-rearing practices. These differences in modelling pattern and rearing practices influence personality characteristics. Several studies conducted in this area show that individual's intellectual development, achievement, motivation, aspiration, self-esteem, and needs and values, anxiety level, adjustment level and other personality characteristics are influenced by socio-class variations.

Though it is not possible to examine all the dimensions of personality and their relation with socio-class conditions, we are to concentrate only on those studies related to adjustment, anxiety and socio-economic status, the three important components of personality which were the objective of this investigation.

The personality is not directly expressed as overt behaviour. Rather it interacts with a situation or series of situations to produce behaviour. These situations consists of more or less complex masses of stimuli that together provoke the personality into responding. Most of the situations in which men operate are social or at least socially mediated. They range in character from such simple circumstances as the casual encounter of man with an acquaintance to such variegated and complex circumstances as that bring a man to attend an elaborate wedding or watch horse rases, or enjoy a film show in a company, or enter into business transactions.

The mere fact that he has reacted in a certain way to a certain situation may mean almost anything so far as his personality is concerned. Only prolonged and detailed study of his behaviour through time and in a great variety of circumstances would enable one to say anything about his personality with any assurance. Even such comparatively simple things as that the man who stole money dislikes to work for it or that the one who goes to the races likes horses or enjoys gambling cannot be said with a feeling of confidence and accuracy.

In a stable society people to get along effectively with the members of their groups, although this is not true in every situation in our own social milieu, the pattern of organization is so much disrupted that deviations from the group norms have become increasingly larger part of the human personality. This fact complicates the matter of person-to-person adjustment and intensifies the difficulties of the social psychologist.

The fact the personality norms vary from society to society and in lesser degree, between different groups within the society is the basis for the layman's crude and unrealistic classification of people into fixed categories; and it is this in turn that underlies many social phenomena. The periodic slaughter of "racial" minorities, the bitterness of a class, and the war of one kind of people upon another kind of people reflect the variation of personality norms among different groups existing in a society.

Culture shifts from generation to generation with Kaleidoscopic variety, and is characterized internally not by uniformity, but by diversity of both individuals and groups, many of whom are in continuous and overt conflict in one sub-system and in active cooperation in another. Culture, as seen from this view point, becomes not so much a superorganic thing suigeneris, but policy, tacitly and gradually concocted by groups of people for the furtherance of their interests; also contract, established by practice, between and among individuals to organize their strivings into mutually facilitating equivalence structure.

Culture also offers many potential enrichments of experience to the individual. This is less apparent to the child, even the adult rarely appreciates the "wisdom of the culture". The culture defines how the different functions, or roles, necessary to group life are to be performed - such roles, for example, as those assigned on the basis of sex and age, or on the basis of membership in a caste, class or occupational group.

In culture and personality analysis, a society is usually considered to be system on a higher level of organization than are the individual organisms, or even the social groups which are the components of that society. Statements about the society—among which are the many statements which constitute a cultural description of it - will be statements about certain properties (including relational properties) of its individual members. Now, if the culturally described system were the only system of which these individuals were components, then a cultural description would be an adequate (for any scientific purpose) description of these several component individuals, and one might well regard society as being logically prior to the individual. But as a matter of fact, individual organisers are also members of system other than their cultural systems. The inter-section of a cultural and non-cultural system, within an individual locus, inevitably generates a third system: the personality system of the individual. This personality relates cultural to other non-cultural systems.

In the case of culture and personality each individual organiser must be considered to be the locus of real personality system, because the states of the organiser relevant to culture are not randomly related to the states of that organiser relevant to a number of other systems.

Relations between intergenerational changes in personality and cultural events outside the maturational cycle are presumably, indicated by the child development process itself. Economic and technological changes, for instance, which occur as the result of rational (Peripheral) motives or of coercive environmental changes, may set in motion other changes which ultimately bring about alterations in child-rearing practices. Thus, intergenerational changes in character can come about via cultural changes which first affect post-infantile experience. Riesman (1950), for instance sees a general relationship between demographic condition, economic process, family structure, and personality structure. In almost all such studies personality is conceived as the dependent variable and economic change as the independent with socialization practices as an intervening variable dependent on economic change. Changes in basic personality, furthermore are usually granted to be very slow and to become noticeable only after efforts to restrain or channel culture changes have failed and after the basic personality has suffered gross and painful distortion under stress.

Cultural changes which increase the heterogeneity of the society, such as acculturation and urbanization, often are believed to pose a serious threat to both personality and social integration (Mead, 1947; Beaglehole 1949). When the culture is "heterogeneous" and rapidly changing there will be a wider variety of personality types produced than in the homogeneous, slowly changing culture. The problem of such a complex society will not be that all of its members will have split personalities, but rather that the problems of socio-cultural organization will exceed the capacities of its members. Under the latter eventuality, many individuals secondarily will experience privation and frustration and come to suffer from psychosomatic and neurotic complaints.

There are two approaches to culture and personality, one emphasizing the replication of uniformities, and the other fostering diversity. Both approaches essay to explain the systems of interaction among individuals by saying something about what goes on inside them. For the purpose of developing empirical support of theoretical analysis of the relation of socio-cultural and personality systems, the second approach which fosters diversity and which is known as the organization of diversity approach is essential. It is generally invoked in the cultural deductive method, which involves subjecting ethnological description to psychological analysis.

In this method, the anthropologist's, historian's or folklorist's accounts of myth and legend, religious ritual, economic relations, and so forth, are "interpreted". The cultural deductive methods treats these behaviours as if they were the neurotic productions of single individual. This has been the particular interest of those culturological psychoanalysts who deduce from the cultural materials, with the help of psychoanalytic theory, the "meaning" of various institutionary to the individual member of the society.

Most of the proponents admit freely that every individual, even in the most uniformitarian society, is somewhat different from every other, as a result of the interplay of various genetic factors and the accidents of experience. But this directly, as it is described, reminds one of the "diversity" of houses in a new development: the point is of different colours and the roof-line rotates from house through a ninety-degree arc, but the floor plans are all the same. In other words, the dynamically important features are assumed to be the ones which are shared. Thus despite lip service to individual variations, the notion of "statistical" distribution is still resisted. Mead, for instance, has insisted that descriptions of individual characteristics and of cultural setting be so precise that perfect co-variations is obtainable between them.

Stemming from Sapir (1949), Mandelbaum (1949) and Hallowell (1957) more than from Mead (1947) and Roheim, (1943) the idea of the uniqueness of an individual gained support from various studies. Like Sapir (1949) Spiro (1951) has emphasized the uniqueness of private family and individual cultures, each as the product as a particular history of social interaction of the individuals.

An alternative is the organizational theory. According to this viewpoint, no population, within a stated cultural boundary, can be assumed to be uniform with respect to any variable or pattern. (For example it cannot be assumed that male and females share the same values, the same role cognitions, the same emotional structure). In every instance, a distribution will be found to characterize the sample. Personality is not assumed to be an internalization of the culture, and culture is not conceptualized as a constant environment, or projection, of all members of the society. Both personality descriptions and cultural descriptions are considered to be intuitive or formal abstractions by an observer from mazeway descriptions of individuals. Individual personality constructs are generalizations about one individual's mazeway over time; culture constructs are generalizations and syntheses of behaviour which are shared by, and or produced by, groups. Model personality and national character are abstractions from personality and cultural data respectively. There is no finite list of categories which defines personality, nor any specified number or proportion of individuals who must share behaviour for it to be called "culture". Descriptions of culture will include statements of relations between behaviour patterns which no informant has given or is able to give; cultural descriptions need not be "Psychologically real" (Wallace & Atkins, 1960) to the informant.

Thus we find, if the microcosmic view is adopted, then research is not necessary to demonstrate that co-variation between personality and culture is exact. The problem becomes essentially one of child development and the question that arises is: how does the child come to "embody" his culture? If the organizational view is adopted, however, then the problem of greater interest is the process by which individually diverse organisms work to maintain, increase, or restore quantity of organization within their own psychological systems and within sociocultural and physical systems of which they are components (Wallace, 1961).

Now, we examine that how the psychological processes affect, and are affected by changes in culture. Anthropologists tend to consider culture change either over very long period of time (macro-temporal change), or over very brief periods of time (micro-temporal change). Macro-temporal processes are frequently labeled cultural evolution and diffusion; micro-temporal processes go by such rubrics as innovation, acculturation, and nativistic movement. Studies of macro-temporal processes of culture change, covering hungered or thousands of years, are generally based on the assumption that "human nature", whatever that is, must be treated as a constant parameter of cultural function, and thus, for all practical purposes, may be ignored. Studies is micro-temporal processes of culture change is more convenient as it covers relatively brief span of time, of the order of few generations or less. Moving equilibrium processes and revitalization processes are two types, relevant for taking into confederation.

The present study is concerned with studying the differences in the personalities of tribal and non-tribal students of Chotanagpur. Hence it would be worth while here to focus attention on the changes which are taking place in the life styles of the tribals of Chotanagpur in the wake of industrial expansion. It is a common place observation to note that the tribals living in the city are slowly but surely taking up a number of urban traits. Acculturation of tribals is a recent phenomenon because of the proliferation of the urban-industries in this tract of Chotanagpur. Since long, the impact of urbanisation on the tribal social life has been in evidence through different factors such as spread of education, contacts with the military for which Ranchi had been one of the headquarters, since the British days spread of Christianity, business and trade, market and the administrative programmes of the Government. In the past, the missionaries were the first to initiate the changes in the old ways of life among the Chotanagpur tribals. Later on, the spread of education among the tribals, the military concentration at Ranchi and the setting-up of important administrative offices of the Bihar Government gave a further push to the tribal social life to change its modes. The basic rural character of the tribals living in Chotanagpur started wilting under the pressures of urbanization and industralization. A large agglomeration of the tribal population in Ranchi in the recent days has brought in its train a host of social problems for the tribals living in this city. Many of the problems are due to the fact that the tribals living in this city are being thrown into such unfamiliar situations which they are unable to combat primarily because they have no prescribed behaviour of such situations in their traditions. As a result of this there has been modifications in their social and cultural values under urban and industrial conditions. Among the tribal youth, however, there is a growing antagonism against their traditional mode of social life, which often results in dropping out or rejecting of tribal modes of behaviour. The non-converted youth are, of course, a little behind this respect. Owing to the complexity of the situations found in an urban community it is not surprising that the urban way of life is slowly but steadily pushing its way into the social pattern of life of the tribals and replacing their traditional ways of the life. This phenomenon which has caught momentum in the recent times, has led to the process of detribalisation in the tribal belt of Chotanagpur. The use of the term "detribalisation" has been made here primarily to indicate the marked change from the tribal to urban standards of behaviour.

Economic Aspect of Family

In the contemporary urban society of the tribals, the wives, in majority of cases, are wage-earners. The majority of men, both among non-converted tribals and converted tribals, expect their wives to contribute to the maintenance of the home. Nearly every well educated woman in a converted tribal family is employed for earning income. A great percentage of non-converted tribal women who have little or no education add to the family's income by doing the work of labourers, or by carrying on trade in a small way such as by selling milk or vegetables grown in a kitchen garden etc. The upkeep of the house and household work are the main activities of the tribal women. Some of them, by force of habit, are still seen collecting fuels for their consumption and grass for sale in the market.

The responsibility of meeting the expenses of the family usually rests upon the male members, especially the master of the house. The grown-up male children and sometimes responsible house-wives also work hard to supplement the family income. With new employment opportunities in urban areas all the elderly members of the family are economic assets.

The variation in behaviour, especially among the converted tribals, reflect the urban ideology of individual initiative and opportunity for self-expression. Among both the non-converted and converted tribals, the behaviour pattern has been modified by the increasing importance of educational attainment, position and wealth.

Many old parents among the non-converted tribals attempt to enforce traditional standards of behaviour upon their children who under the urban influences attempt to avoid obeying them as far as possible. Such variation in behaviour is associated with the length of urban residence, intensity of contact with urban culture, economic and educational status and then the influence of an individual member. The variation in behaviour, especially among the converted tribals, reflects the urban ideology of individual initiative and opportunity for self-expression.

The fact that majority of the married women contribute to the family income has given the womenfolk an economic standard which has been a major factor in raising their status. The increased freedom and individualisation of the family, more strongly observed among the converted tribals and their release from the strict supervision of the traditional rural neighborhood more markedly found among the non-converted tribals have given rise to family instability. There are evidences to believe that a modified form of conjugal relationship in which romantic love, democratic companionship and equal responsibility are important elements, are emerging among the tribals of Ranchi.

Urban-bred children are sophisticated, frequently more literate and have greater mastery of the new urban environment than their parents. The parents find that the playground, the cinema and street life in general are the effective forces moulding the development of their children. Lack of schooling of the non-converted tribal children and lack of appropriate employment opportunities for both the converted and non-converted tribals are factors which the produce an indisciplined and maladjusted tribal youths (Vidyarthi, 1964).

The above observations make it clear that the tribal families are undergoing severe stresses in transition from rural to urban environment and adaptation to industrial economy.

Marriage

The marriage rate is too high and the extent of high figure at once suggests that the custom of marriage has not fallen back owing to urban impact. However, in case of converted tribals, the age of marriage of girls and boys has been found much higher than that of boys and girls of the non-converted tribals. Among the converted tribals among whom the age of marriage both for male and female remain high is due to their coming in contact with the church which discourages marriage at an earlier age.

Among the non-converted tribals, though marriage is still celebrated under tribal custom, there is a wide range of variations in the procedure. Church conducts the marriage of the converted tribal boys and girls. Civil marriage has not been recorded among the non-converted tribals. Among the converted tribals, however, a few cases of civil marriage has been recorded but it is extremely rare.

Marriage has become a costly affair for the tribals also. Inclusion of more pomp and show due to urban influence by hiring of loudspeaker, by taking of the bride-room on rickshaw or taxi to bride's house, etc. costs them much. The bride price, in case on non-converted tribals has, however, become reduced to some extent. Formerly it was fixed to a maximum of 12 pieces of cloth (Khand) and rupees twenty five to rupees thirty. But now, due to change in outlook only cash is demanded and that too only up to a maximum of rupees twenty five to hundred.

Generally monogamy is the rule. *Sorurate* and *Levirate* marriages have also been recorded but the percentage of such marriage is very insignificant. Widow marriage, however, has been reported in a fair percentage. Incidence of separating and divorce is relatively low in the city in comparison to the conditions in rural areas. Inter-tribal marriages are quite uncommon among the non-converted tribals. However, three such cases have been reported among converted tribals. It is interesting to note that a good number of cases of marriage between tribals and non-tribals have occurred. Nearly all such marriages continued to be successful. The men who married tribal girls were either Hindu or Muslim. Among the tribal brides or bridegrooms, majority were converted tribals.

Association

While on the one hand traditional association of the tribals are weakening under urban way of life, some of the urbanite tribals on the other hand, due to the influence of city life exerted on them, join those who have similar interests to obtain their ends. In the traditional tribal society it is generally possible to predict their way of life on the basis of less variation in human behaviour. In almost every relationship in the city, the general pattern of group formation and affiliation is not so clear.

The planned efforts on the economic front have hardly touched the fringe of the tribal problems. The vast majority of the tribal population still remain at a point where they had been before. The prevalence of poverty and inequality, virtually unchanged over the year can be seen most clearly in the conditions of life of the two disadvantaged groups in our society, "the scheduled castes and the scheduled tribes" (Draft Five Year Plan, 1978). The social infrastructure created during the planning were mainly shared by the affluent section of the two groups and the sufferings of the lower strata of the tribals increased manifold. This has happened because the aspirations of the tribals have increased very fast as a result of the working of the demonstration effect in the fast changing social complex of hitherto sleepy tribal society of the plateau-hills and the villages. Industrialization has changed the geo-ecological balance in the tribal region of Bihar and the inner urge for the economic betterment in the tribal society has become so prominent that it requires a special treatment which may suit their age-old socio-psychological tradition.

The tribals numbering 49 lakhs, account for 8.75 per cent of the total 564 lakhs population of this state. Thus the tribals form an important segment in the total demographic structure of Bihar. They have a deep concentration in the five districts of south Bihar. Table 1.1 gives the figure.

Table 1.1 : Demographic Structure of the Tribal Region of Bihar (1971 census)

Distribution with Area	*Total Population*	*Tribal Population*
Bihar (the whole state) (173,876 km.)	56,353,369	4,932,767
Ranchi (18,331 km.)	2,611,445	1,516,698
Santhal Parganas (19,129 km.)	3,186,908	1,154,281
Singhbhum (13,447 km.)	2,437,799	1,124,317
Hazaribagh (18,060 km.)	3,020,214	331,791
Palamu (12,677 km.)	1,504,350	287,150

Thus the above table makes it clear that the highest population of the tribals is in Ranchi district, closely followed by Santhal Parganas and Singhbum. There is comparatively thinner tribal population in Hazaribagh and Palamu districts. This tribal region is well endowed with natural gifts and possesses immense potentialities for modern growth, though the tribal people live in this region with their aborigine socio-cultural traditions.

The tribal regions are located in the Southern part of Bihar, where about one third of the populating (32.12 per cent) are of aboriginal tribes. Many other characteristics of this part of the state is figured in Table 1.2.

Table 1.2 : Selected sub-regional Data of Bihar

Region	*Density of Rural Popula-tion*	*Percentage of Urban Popula-tion to total population*	*Percentage of Litera-cy*	*Percentage of Sch. Tribes*	*Percentage of Area*
Southern	153	16.01	20.39	32.12	8.68
Northern	469	4.99	16.91	0.79	14.62
Central	359	11.98	23.67	0.96	41.76

Source : Draft Five Year Plan (1978–83) p. 113.

The above table indicates that the southern part (the tribal region) of the state possesses the high percentage of the scheduled tribes (32.12) with the high percentage of urban population (16.01) to total population and lower in density of rural population, with poor irrigation facilities in comparison to the other part of the state. The modern industries have clustered round this region because of the availability of the rich minerals, but have failed to uplift the lot of the poor tribals. On the other hand, it has created an artificial economic demarcation between the poor tribals on the one hand and the elite and affluent tribals and non-tribals on the other. The influx of non-tribal population and increase of a class of elite tribals are the by-product of the modern industrialisation of Bihar. This has practically aggravated the socio-psychological tension in the tribals. The recent wave of industrialization has not influenced the village economy and vast majority of the tribals have either adopted farming and agriculture or engaged themselves as labourers and wage-earners in urban areas. Nevertheless, they come back to their original folk, though they vastly differ among themselves so far as their socio-cultural situation is concerned.

A discussion of tribal population in Bihar is incomplete without the discussion of tribals of Chotanagpur, as the largest number of tribal population of Bihar live in this region. The region is rich in mines and forests. It is full of variety of minerals and particularly famous for coal and irons. Even the precious goods as uranium and mica are found in this region. The hills and mountains, the steep landscape, numerous rivers and other natural resources have endowed this area with the potentiality to grow as an industrialized belt. No wonder, therefore, that in the post-independence era the Government of India has given a special preference to industries of Chotanagpur region. Bokaro Steel City and Heavy Engineering Corporation, Hatiya can be named in this connection.

Most of the tribal population of Chotanagpur zone live in villages and depend on agriculture. The main crop is paddy. But they also have some economic gains from forests. They product country liquor from mahua flowers and also collect some wages by selling "Tendu Patta (leaf)". By and large the village life of the tribals is very impoverished.

The region of Chotanagpur remained cut off from the rest of the world due to the geographical reasons. Formerly there were no road links and other means for communication. Hill tops, steep slopes and dense forests made this area difficult to be approached. And thus, the tribals of this region maintained their tribal identity for a long time. But in the sixteenth century the Hindu elements entered this tribal belt. And in the nineteenth century the European missionaries infiltrated into this region during the British rule. Gradually, the influence of Hindu elements and Christian missionaries began to change the social structure of tribal people, ushering in a period of improvement in communication, education and rapid industrialization in post independent era. The change in this social and cultural structure of tribal society have become more apparent today. More specifically the acculturation has been brought about by the following means:

1. Impact of Hinduism on tribal culture
2. Impact of Christianity
3. Adivasi Seva Kendra (Adimjati Sewa Mandal)
4. Statutory provisions
5. Urbanization in the area of Chotanagpur

1. Impact of Hindu Culture on Tribal Population of Chotanagpur

Chotanagpur, though predominantly occupied by different tribes, is also inhabited by Hindus. They are called by the Tribes as 'Sudh' or 'Sudhan ! The word 'Diku' is used for the Hindu which means an outsider.

The impact of Hinduism is discernible on most of the minor tribes of Chotanagpur. Many of the tribes like the Cheros, the Kharwars, Rajwars, Ranhas, Kisans and others have been very much influenced by Hinduism. They have incorporated a number of Hindu manners and customs. They call themselves Hindu and practice Hindu customs. As a result, they have acquired a definite social status in traditional caste system of Hinduism. Even the major tribes as Mundas and Oraon, who are maintaining their tribal individuality to a great extent, have failed to spare themselves from the influence of Hinduism. Most of the Munda and Oraon tribes who are near the Hindu villages have adopted Hindu practices without knowing their true nature. Due to the influence of Hinduism, many of tribal clans Hindu Gods and Goddesses like Mahadev, Devi Mai Kali etc. Not only this some of the tribals also employ Hindu priests on certain religious occassions. The most important impact of Hindu culture on tribal population is seen in Hindu-type socio-religious movement. The Munda 'Sheoli, Dharamand Birsa Dharma and Beshneo Bhagat' and 'Tana Bhagat' in Oraon can be equated with different religious groups of Hindu saints such as 'Kabir Panth', "Arya Samaj", "Gorya Sampradai" etc.

2. Impact of Christianity"

The tribals of Chotanagpur have been greatly influenced by Christian missionaries. The main aim of these Christian missionaries was to propagate the Christianity in tribes and increase the number of converts. To achieve this aim these Christian missionaries have done a lot of social services for the aboriginals living in remote forest areas. The missionary have taken great pains to open schools and health centres in such remote forest areas which were difficult to approach. Among the different types of social service, the contributions done in education of tribal people by these missionaries is most significant. Sachindanad (1964) has rightly observed "education has been one of the biggest achievements of the Christian Mission even in the most interior parts of Chotanagpur. Most of the tribal leaders of today have been educated in Mission schools. Education has, therefore, given them not only literacy, but enlightenment in all aspects of life. It has opened up a vast horizon for getting post in Government service and elsewhere. Those who took advantage of these facilities have been able to enhance their social status in the eyes of not only their followers but also in those of the non-tribals". Singh (1989) has observed, "Christianity has brought good changes, literacy is one of them. Thus it is obvious that the Christian Missionaries have done a great job in educating and making all round development of the tribal people, of course, at the cost of their traditional religion. The missions have influenced the life and behaviours of these tribal people". Several studies conducted on tribal and non-tribal population show that education brought to tribals by these missionaries has raised their aspirations and achievement motivation. Bardiyar (1987) has also found differences in the personality characteristics of Christian and non-Christian Mundas. Singh (1987) in his study has found higher political orientation in tribal students. As Singh (1981) observed in his study that the tribal aborigine was altogether different with definitely a wider outlook on life. Generally raised in social scale, he was liberated from the old tribal taboos. He had an increased sense of responsibility and self respect both as an individual and as a race.

3. Adimjati Seva Mandal

To celebrate the 'Annual Function of the Congress Party' some top leaders like Mahatma Gandhi, Dr. Rajendra Prasad and others comped at Ramgarh. They got there the opportunity to see the pitiable conditions of the tribal pople. Moved by their simplicity and painful life, these leaders decided to establish a 'Seva Kendra' for these poor tribal mass. The Seva Kendra was later changed to 'Adimjati Seva Mandal'. Some of the young selfless social workers of the time like Narayanji, Bhaiyaram Munda, Manki Singhraj Singh, Pyarelal Kerketta and many others took the challenge of educating the tribals of this area and they started their work in right earnest. But the work of the Mandal suffered a lot due to the negative attitude of the British Government. But by 1952-53 the Seva Mandal work became popular in the tribal localities. Several schools were opened by the Seva Mandal but in the year 1963-64 they were nationalized, and with this the 'Adimjati Seva Kendra' was adversely affected but the services done by the Mandal in bringing social changes in tribal areas is indeed considerable.

4. Statutory provisions for Scheduled Castes and Scheduled Tribes

Statutory provisions in the Constitution of India have brought a lot of changes in the social, cultural and economic life of tribal people. The tribals in India have remained backward due to two rasons - (i) Their isolation from the geneal society, (ii) and their exploitations by non-tribals. To protect the tribal's interest and accelerate their standard of life, seveal provisions have been made in the Constitution. Article 46 of the Constitution provides "The state shall promote with speical care the educational and economic interests of the weaker sections of the people and in particular and Scheduled Castes and Scheduled Tribes and shall protest them from social injustice and all forms of exploitations." Under the fifth schedule of the Constitution it provides for establishment of 'A Tribes Advisory Council' to advise on the matters of tribal welfare and advancement of the tribals of the state. Articles 330, 332 and 334 of the Constitution provides for the reservation of seats for Scheduled Tribes in the Lok Sabha and Vidhan Sabha of the various states. These provisions provide political facilities to the weaker section in the democractic world.

In accordance with the Article 164 of the Constitution a Minister for Tribal Welfare is appointed for Bihar, Madhya Pradesh and Orissa. The Minister incharge of the Tribal Welfare has to look after the interest of tribals and has to promote with special care the educational and economic interests of the tribals.

Thus, we see that in post-independent India, the policies of the Government have been in nature of 'Protective Discrimination' towards the weaker sections. In the field of economic upliftment measurement such as allotment of lands, house sites, building materials and other monetary aid have been taken by the State Government. The Government has rightly recognized the needs of the SCs and STs in the field of education. The State and Union Government have adopted several policies to eradicate the educational backwardness from Scheduled Castes and Scheduled Tribes. In the agricultural area also the State Government has started several programmes as supply of improved seeds, manures, agriculture tools, allocation of funds for establishing poultry and fisheries etc.

In the area of communication several roads and bridges over rivers have been constructed by the State and Central Government. There are still many roads and bridges under construction. The roads have linked the remote villages to the nearby towns. These roads have certainly increased the communication. This has facilitated the tribal population to come in contact with the non-tribals. Other facilities as health centres, child-care centres, maternity centres have been raised for the health services of tribal people.

5. Urbanisation

The factor which has most influenced the socio-cultural set-up in the tribal area of Chotanagpur is its fast pace of urbanization. Several urban areas and townships have developed in the post-independence years. Ranchi, Dhanbad, Jharia, Bokaro and Jamshedpur are now considered as among the highly industrialized cities in India.

The reasons for the growth of urbanization-big and small townships-is the potentiality of this belt in varieties of minerals, coal and iron ores. The important minerals found in plenty in this area, have attracted both the private and public sectors to raise industries. Bokaro Steel City, Heavy Engineering Corporation, Jamshedpur Steel City may be named under heavy industrial projects. Aluminium alloy factory in Moori and several other semi-government projects may be named as major industrial complex. These big and small factories have generated development of townships. Further, coal and other mine industries in themselves have contributed to the fast extension of town areas.

Urbanization has allowed and attracted the tribals living in remote villages to seek jobs in towns and thus, a large number of tribal population has migrated to towns. There they do not only get educational facilities but they come also in contact with non-tribal people. The urbanization has not improved only the economic status of tribals but it has also helped them awaken their intellectual and non-intellectual abilities. It has also influenced the traditional habits of tribals (Bardiyar, 1987). Actually urbanization has increased the social mobility in Chotanagpur region. The industrial towns are providing tribal mass education, job as well as contact with non-tribal people. Due to these factors a significant change in the socio-cultural life of these tribal people is perceptible there. We can see there the tribal women dressing themselves in sari and blouse and tribal youths eating in hotels and visiting cinema halls. These industrial cities, thus, have done a lot to change the fortune of these poor tribals. Several studies conducted in this area show that tribal youths living in urban areas also aspire for better jobs. They have also high achievement motivation. They have been found exhibiting higher intellectual abilities (Bardiyar, 1987).

The urbanization has affected the cultural values of tribals in this area. The urbanization is also bringing changes in the jungle habits of tribals. Netting fishes, hunting animals etc. are being replaced by other hobbies and recreations. There is also seen a perceptible change in the religious festivity of tribal people. They also errect shamiyana and use loudspeakers blaring film songs in their festivals. We can see tribals riding bikes and wearing up-to-date clothes. Thus the tribals are gradually breaking from their traditional systems in favour of modernization. Even the illiterate tribals like to work in factories as unskilled workers and live in towns rather than to stick to their nomadic life. Thus we see that the tribals of Chotanagpur region have been influenced socio-economically by various social factors operating there. These factors have brought a lot of changes in the culture and behaviour pattern of tribals.

Prior to Industrialization and Modernization there were great differences between the tribals and non-tribals. There was a time when the tribals lived a semi-nomadic life, always on the move in search of food. Later, their life, philosophy and thinking, their rites and rituals were practically centered on different agricultural activities. Hunting, fishing and food-gathering though subsidiary, were considered important sources of subsistence. They used tree-barks, tree-leaves and animal spins to cover their body. They often ate raw meat and had no permanent dwellings. The tribals had a lot of taboos and superstitions. Their belief in witchcraft was strong, sometimes leading even to murder in the name of sacrifice to appease an angry divinity. In those days, barter system has a common feature of day-to-day transactions. Since the language of the tribals was confined to their own tribe, they found it very difficult to mix with the non-tribals. They could not converse or communicate with people not belonging to their tribe. Due to this inferiority complex often seized them and as such they often escaped from other tribal groups as well as the non-tribals.

Industrialization, modernisation, impact of Hinduism on tribal culture, impact of Christianity, work done by Adivasi Seva Kendra, statutory provisions in the Constitution etc. have created a situation in which the tribals have made attempts to adjust themselves. Though, these have made considerable impact on the tribals yet tribalism has not been swept off by the flood tide of industrialization. Turning of tribals into the industrial proletariat has not radically changed their personality. Adaptation of changes is always prompted by the environmental effects.

In summary it may be said that modernization, urbanization and the effect of cross-cultural interactions have considerably changed the functioning of the life-style of the tribals. The Christian missionaries have done some good work in the tribal region of Bihar which have directly aroused an eco-political awareness among the non-christian tribals. It is because of these social developments that the tribal society of post independent India suffers more from the intra-tribal conflict and exploitation than from inter-tribal social exploitations. The intra-tribal conflict and disparity is more serious in the modern tribal society of Bihar than inter-tribal disparity. Hence creation of a socio-psychological environment for the betterment of the common tribals is required.

A society includes the organized population of people living together and sharing a mutual sense of belongingness. Each society exposes its members to certain cultural influences, that is, it transmits certain attitudes, ideas, norms, standards, their anxiety level, adjustment, values, beliefs, practices and modes of behaviours to the coming generations. This cultural transmission is called "social heritance". But in every socio-cultural society we see social-class differences. We see upper, lower and middle class in each socio-cultural group.

We have already seen in the previous pages that social classes influence the personality growth, and the members of the advantaged the disadvantaged socio-class vary in their personality characteristics. We have also seen in the previous pages that anxiety and adjustment of the individuals are shaped according to the socio-class to which they belong. As the purpose of the present study was to see the development of anxiety score and adjustment level in tribal students, therefore, the tribal students were grouped on the basis of the social classes to which they belonged. As the tribal societies of India have also gone through several changes due to education and other modernization processes, it is expected that there will be differences in the anxiety level and adjustment level of different tribal groups.

On the basis of above discussion it emerges that beside the personality patterns there might be differences in adjustment capacity and anxiety level of tribals and non-tribals. The study has been undertaken to investigate possible differences in these areas. But before to deal with methodology and the results of this study let us examine the dimensions of this study in some detail.

Adjustment

It is the name given to a very general process in which an individual changes his response patterns or aspect of his environment They are basically of two types: attack and withdrawal. Some individuals, when confronted with problems, do nothing. Psychologists tend to feel that the second type of adjustment-withdrawal is much less desirable than the former. As a result of good adjustment, tension is relieved or eliminated. This does not happen in the withdrawal process. The original problem does not become solved. New problems arise through the individual's withdrawal. Daydreaming, sulking, feigning illness and the like are samples of this type of behaviour.

The term adjustment may be used to imply the process by which a person changes his behaviour to achieve a harmonious relation between himself and his environment. Life may be looked upon as a long series of adjustments in which the individual is constantly adjusting himself to the demands of the external environment as well as to the needs of his physiological and mental constitution. The individual is continually eating and drinking, seeking shelter and affection, seeking approval and friends, security and prestige. The adjustments he makes are not always healthy, sound or effective from the point of view of his lifelong welfare but they are made as they seem at the moment to satisfy some of his needs.

Adjustments may be defined as a process by which the individual maintains a level of physiological and psychological balance or equilibrium between his needs and the circumstances that influence the satisfaction of those needs. Some psychologists define adjustments as behaviour directed to the reduction of tension. This means that adjustment is a matter of interaction between the individual and his environment. Any attempt for adjustment reflects how far his capacities can cope with the demands of his environment. A well-adjusted individual is one who has come to terms with his environment, that is, one who has reached harmony in his relations with his environment. But adjustment is not a static condition. It is relative and temporary. The individual is for ever facing problems and devising ways and means to meet them. This needs and environments keep changing and he is for ever seeking adjustments. A student need a job and works hard to qualify for it. When he gets it he is satisfied, and there is harmony in his relations with his environment. But this harmony does not last long. Soon he is anxious to make got at his job and excel his colleagues or to seek another more remunerative job. So his needs and problems never leave him and continue to disturb his adjustments.

This harmony and contentment may mislead one to accept that the wastrel is adjustment to his wasteful ways even as the poor are to slum living or the vagabond to useless wanderings. So in considering adjustment we have to ask to what condition and pattern of environment the individual is expected to be adjusted. Discontent, lack of adjustment and complacency, needs and motives leading to tension and disharmony, and all those factors producing or increasing anxiety and spurring the individual on the struggle and learn more appropriate behaviour in meeting his needs and problems are therefore to be welcomed. The child who withdraws from reality and surrenders himself to excessive day-dreaming or the one who satisfies his hunger for superiority by bragging and boasting should be made to realize the inadequacy of his present behaviour and adjustment so that he seeks more adequate ways of behaving and adjusting to his needs and problems. According to Kisker (1972) personality adjustment indicates how well a particular individual has been able to cope with himself and with the environment around him. A person is considered to be well adjusted if he accepts himself, and the ways of life he has to follow, without getting into trouble. In a similar vein Coleman (1976) defines adjustment as: "Effectiveness of the individual's efforts to meet his needs and to adopt to environment", commenting upon the dynamic nature of adaptation/adjustment, White (1959) says, "The concept of adjustment implies the constant interaction between individual and environment, each making demands on the other, in most cases adjustment is compromise between them."

The word adjustment has been used with different connotations and we shall try to review them. The biologists use the word adaptation in place of adjustment. They confine the word to environmental adaptation that the organisms have to make. In this sense adaptation is a simple process in as much as the complexity that social interactions give rise to, is not there in the environmental adaptation made by an organism.

The social scientists are mainly concerned with that aspect of adjustment which the individual has to make in social situation. In this sense adjustment means conformity or non-conformity with the social norms. In other words adjustment refers to the relationship that exists between an individual and his or her environment, especially the social environment in the satisfaction of his or her motives.

As per psycho-analytical approach adjustment means an effective adjustment made by ego between demands of Id and restrictions imposed by super-ego. It is also defined in terms of freedom from tension, feelings of inner well being and adapting onself to the needs of other individuals. According to Bolding, et al., (1956) "Adjustment is a process by which a living organism maintains a balance between its needs and the circumstances that influence the satisfaction of those needs".

Psychologically speaking, adjustment means a harmonious balance between an individual on one side and his biological and socio-cultural needs/demands on the other. In this way adjustment of a person may be defined as the characteristic way in his life or solves the main problems of his life. Adjustment therefore is directly connected with needs and problems of life and refers to the behaviour patterns through which those needs are satisfied or problems are solved habitually. It is obvious that everyone at all times is confronted with needs and problems and therefore he must acquire an adequate need-satisfying or problem-solving behaviour. It is equally obvious that such behaviour must be consistent with the standard, customs and more prevailing values in the community in which the individual lives. Unless he does that he may find himself in conflict with the social order and instead of solving his problems he may multiply them.

The main problems of life may be classified under three heads: (1) Problems arising from bodily and physical needs, those connected with food, shelter, housing, protection from physical hazards, and the like; (2) problems arising from psychological needs, the need for comfort, satisfaction and freedom from pain, the need for approval, independence, self-esteem, success and achievement, and the need for security, affection and regard of our fellow beings and sense of belongingness; (3) problems arising from the socio-cultural environment in which he lives, the social custom and taboos, the social demands and prohibitions, the conflicts and contradictions inherent in our society and culture. The severity of the adjustment problem will depend upon the intensity and strength of the need which is being denied satisfaction, the extent to which the need is being denied, the extent to which it affects the satisfaction of other urgent and basic needs, the potentialities of the person to stand the strain of tension and weather difficulties, the extent to which environment favours need-satisfaction, his self concept influencing his awareness of the frustration of his needs and his social feeling that the satisfaction of his needs does not interfere with the fulfillment of the legitimate needs of others.

Adjustment does not mean passive acceptance of the influences and forces of environment. Nor does it imply and surrender or twist of one's personality, attitudes and values to obtain harmony with, conflict or thwarting factors in or outside one's mental makeup. It implies active interaction with, or participation in the environmental changes and influences. In solving serious problems or fulfilling urgent basic needs the individual marshals all his resources and does his best. No doubt, in this participation he influence others in the group and is himself influenced by others but his adjustments are marked by active participation, acceptance of responsibility and achieving goals. Good adjustment is the relative term. What is good adjustment for one individual may be exceedingly bad for another. Perhaps in the final analysis, it is just how the individual himself feels about his adjustment that makes it good or bad. Adjustment then is relative and individual, and of course, related to the culture in which one lives. An examination of the customs and beliefs of other people, such as Eskimos, south sea Islanders, or Japanese, shows the differences in so called 'normal' adjustments in different cultures. What mould lead to arrest in one culture in a daily way of living in another. A basic approach to evaluating adjustment is, then, the interpretation of an individual's behaviour in the light of how he feels about it. Perhaps a large part of this whole process has to be self evaluated. That all psychologists are not in accord about the importance of every one's being well adjusted is evidenced by Linton (1945), whose view is that real progress is brought about by people who are maladjusted and not conforming in their habits. Inspite of all we have just said, the growth and development of an individual's personality becomes one of the most important objectives of the school.

The organs of the human body are classified into two chief groups, according to whether they (1) function internally to maintain the individual's health and growth or (2) function in the individual's activities in the environment as he overcomes obstacles to the satisfaction of his needs. The first group, called the organs of maintenance, includes the heart and blood vessels, the lungs, the ailmentary canal and its digestive glands and the liver. The second group, known as the organs of adjustment, includes the muscles, the skeleton, and certain glands.

"Adjustment to inner and outer demands is a continuing and never completed process", (Ruch, 1970). The term "adjustment" has two meanings. In one sense it is a continual process by which a person varies his behaviour to produce to more harmonious relationship between himself and his environment. In another sense adjustment is a state, i.e., the condition of harmony arrived at by a person when we call "well adjusted" (Gates, Jersild, McConnel, Challman, 1971).

The adjustment inventory provides measures of adjustment in four areas, viz:

(A) Home adjustment

(B) Social adjustment

(C) Health and Emotional adjustment

(D) School/College adjustment

(A) Home Adjustment

The person who lives in family and obeys all family members his father and mother give respect to him. His brothers and sisters adjust with him and play with each other. The person who takes breakfast and dinner with his family is called "good adjustment" at home. When the person does not get respect from his family and does not play with his brothers and sisters it is called "bad adjustment" at home.

(B) Social Adjustment

. The commonly accepted definition of social adjustment is "The changes is habitual conduct or behaviour which an individual must make in order to fit into community in which he lives" Saul, L. J. et al. (1937).

All persons live in society. The society has some rules and regulations. The persons who follows the laws and regulations of society his social adjustment is good, otherwise it is not good.

(C) Health and Emotional Adjustment

Every person has blood, fat and strength etc. who has good health and takes interest in many social and emotional activities his health and emotional adjustment is good. The person who is week and his ideas are bad, mostly that person suffers from many diseases and his health and emotional adjustment is bad.

(D) School/College Adjustment

After sometime infants grow and understand about alphabets and vocabulary. They go to school to take education. The teachers give them knowledge and the children listen them. Those students who take more interest in school/college activities give respect to teachers and obey to all members of the institution, are called good adjusted in school/college. In other way, those students who do not give respect to teachers and other staff are called bad adjusted in school/college.

A Typical Adjustments

Marked peculiarities of individual experience may, however, result in adjustments that deviate so far from the typical that the individual stands out in striking contrast to his fellows.

Those who fail to make a heterosexual adjustment to the problems of sex life, those who are so much mal-prepared for marital adjustment that they never succeed in marrying, those who have been prepared to make their livelihood only in anti legal ways, those who have failed to make any occupational adjustment and have turned to the life of the open road, etc. are persons who have made a typical adjustments.

Whatever the tribals have gained in the wake of industrialization and other processes of modernization has been possible because of their constant attempts at adjustment at various levels. A large number of tribal groups remained withdrawn from the new issues facing them. But some who responded to them actively achieved new heights of progress Even those who in the beginning remained withdrawn later on, saw the benefits of actively adjusting themselves to new changes. These factors contributed to the acquisition of new modern values by the tribals.

The tribals followed the time-tested principle of social, cultural, physical adjustment. Despite all attempts to bring about adjustment at various levels the tribals have still not allowed their culture and traditions to be swept aside. They still cling to them. They are conscious of acquiring new values to live in the complex world which we have today. But they still feel that they must retain their tribal identity. On the basis of what we have seen in the foregoing paragraphs, we can safely conclude that there are definite differences between the tribals and non-tribals. So far every help to be given to them for their amelioration, a specific strategy suited to them has to be hit upon.

Anxiety

Anxiety for the purpose of this study has been operationally defined in terms of the drive-level, as such high anxious individuals are expected to have better academic achievement. However, investigators have obtained conflicting results. There is a group of investigators (Biggs, 1959; Furneaux, 1957; Lundin and Swayer, 1965; Lynn, 1957; Robinson, 1966; Terman and Taylor, 1954) who have reported a positive relationship between anxiety and academic achievement. On the contrary, in a number of studies conducted in India and outside the country (Blumberg and Schmidt, 1970; Brar, 1970; Cown, Zax, Klein, Izzo and Trost, 1965; Feldhusen, Denny and Candon, 1965; Frost, 1965; Hazari and Thakur, 1970; Kawkes and Furst, 1971; Keller and Rowley, 1964; Kraft, 1969; Lott and Lott, 1968; Lunneborg, 1964; Pandit, 1970; Parsons, Morris and Denny, 1963; Patel and Joshi, 1972; Raphelson, 1957; Sarason, S.B.et al 1958, Sassenrath, 1967; Sexena, 1965; Singal, 1974; Singh, 1971; Singh, 1976; Sinha, 1966; Sinha, 1972; Shanker and Brar, 1973) either a negative or an insignificant relationship between anxiety and academic achievement has been recorded. Sharma (1970) has reported that subjects who are very low and very high on manifest anxiety are poorer in school achievement than the middle group. Merryman (1974) has also reported that moderate anxiety group is significantly superior to high anxiety group on comprehension and vocabulary tasks. However, in some of these studies (Gokulanathan, 1971; Dubey, 1976; Nijhawan, 1968) high anxious subjects have been shown to have better achievement and in some others (Merryman, 1974; Sinha, 1970; Sinha, 1972; Stevenson and Iscoe, 1956) it has been reported that low anxious subjects are better achievers.

Now the question is whether the tribal and non-tribal students differ in terms of their anxiety scores or not? Gokulnathan (1971) has found no difference between tribals and non-tribals with regards to their achievement related anxiety levels. However. Sharaf and Singh (1977) have maintained that tribals are more anxious than non-tribals. Thus it is obvious that the two findings contradict each other. Besides on the basis of the findings of only two studies is difficult to generalize the results. Therefore, in the present investigation, the purpose is to investigate that whether tribal and non-tribal school students differ significantly in terms of their anxiety-level.

Meyer, W.J. et al., (1962) in a study showed that educational streaming of general and test anxiety scales were administered to 266 children attending 4th and 5th grades. The children had been subdivided into superior and inferior subgrades on the basis of their performance in first 3 grades. 3 hypothesis were tested. The correlation between the 2 scales would be positive, the correlation between subgrade level and test anxiety would be negative, and general anxiety scores would be independent of educational streaming practices. The results were consistent with these expectations.

Moore (1965) also found some definite indications of anxiety reactions and depression among high school students who had migrated to urban areas. Not only this, but on the basis of his investigations, he found significant increases in depression, sadness, dissatisfaction with life situation, feelings of being misunderstood, and feelings of loneliness as the boy grows older. More than half, the students were found to be moody, depressed, and worried over studies, and many felt that they are not understood by parents, teachers and friends. In a study Singh and Singh (1977) shows a dualistic viewpoint on anxiety. At last he discussed anxiety is summation of unrealized aggressive energies.

Aggression is related to frustration of drives of every nature.

Hallowell (1949) regards anticipated frustration as a determinant of anxiety. He attempts to point out common elements in both views by (a) stating and elaborating the hypothesis that anticipated frustration is a sufficient condition for anxiety arousal, and (b) identifying frustration with the two factors of drive and adaptive lack. In the British Journal of educational Psychology, Banretic and Meadows (1965) discussed about interest mental health and attitudinal correlates of academic achievement among university students. In the Journal of Education Psychology, published by American Psychological association, Mattsson (1974) discussed about, personality traits associated with effective teaching in rural and urban schools. Saxena (1981) has done the work about reactions to frustrations needs of adjustment and vocational interests of the super normals, normals and subnormals.

Singh and Kumar (1977) in a study shows the effects of manifest anxiety on the academic achievement of collage students. In this he found that the students of low intellectual ability had low anxiety scores. For the very superior students however, anxiety appeared to facilitate academic performance.

Hodapp (1978) found that high school students were administered 2 anxiety scales, that test anxiety scale and need for achievement scale. Scores on these tests were related to scores on the school and collage ability test (Scat). Test anxiety was found to be negatively correlated with Scat scores. The negative correlations obtained tended to be, larger for female than for male subjects. The need for achievement scale showed only a slight tendency to correlate negatively with Scate Scores. The results were interpreted as being consistent with normal adolescents.

All of us, are molded, from the cradle to the grave, by the ways, habits, customs and the whole culture around us. There is however, some environmental forces that affect the development of the individuals. In other words personality develops from the interaction of the living human organism with an environment that frustrates or encourages and conditions its impulses. Psycho-analysts have shown how the manner of early handling, feeding and weaning, the love and security that the parents may give or withhold and the 'sanctions' that society imposes mould the growing child. Thus personality is moulded and profound by the very nature of the culture (Joshi & Tiwari, 1977; Kulshrestha, 1968; Tripathi, 1977).

If then, we wish to understand what the social surroundings do to the molding of action, feeling and thought in the growing individual, and the way in which the relationships among persons constitute the supporting and stimulating pressures which make us so different from people who grow up in other social worlds.

Thus it is going to be our task to look at the relations between the individual and his culture. In bringing up children wisely, and guiding them into suitable educational careers and occupations, we have to take account of their personal qualities.

The problem of an investigation into personality dimensions of school pupils is usually helpful for teacher and important for the country. Unlike the carpenter, or farmer, or financier we cannot merely look and see that we have been doing. Like the ocean navigator, on the contrary, we must take the trouble to find out what we are and how we are. In other words what sort of person we are and how we interact with each other in delay life situations. How and what constitutional-situational determinants influence the growth of personality.

Personality are alike in certain aspects and different in others. They differ slightly in some ways and greatly in others. Again there is difference of opinion. There are some who put emphasis on what is common to all and there are others who put emphasis on what is unique to an individual. This difference of opinion is the difference of American *versus* German conceptions of personality. As Allport (1951) has pointed out that American Psychologists have been concerned with a nomothetic approach to problems of personality almost to the exclusion of idiographic considerations. Nomothetic approach puts emphasis on what is common to all, whereas, idiographic approach puts emphasis on what is unique to the personality of individual. The concept of personality generally connotes not only an organization of motives, but also a repertoire of cognitive process. Contemporary dynamic psychology, in contrast to the early Freudian is very much concerned with these "ego functions", for they provide the "organization factor" (Rashkis, 1957) which makes the difference between the intricate emotional architecture of mental health and the shambles of mental illness. Further more, these cognitive or ego, functions govern the individual's relation to the world around him via perception, learning, language and other forms of symbolic communication and by "insightful creative" or "imaginative" restructuring. Thus cognitive processes both organize the motives of the individual and relate them to his environment.

The Purpose of the Study

We have seen in the previous pages that the tribals of Bihar, particularly of Chotanagpur region have been stimulated to various socio-cultural change by the forces operating in the region. We have discussed several forces such as the impact of Hindu culture, statutory provisions and economic aids by the Central and State Government, urbanization, and industrialization as forces bringing change in their lives.

We have also discussed that personality characteristics of an individual are influenced by the scale-class to which he belongs. Studies conducted in this area very clearly show that persons of advantaged class posses more desirably characteristic (Chopra, 1967; Sharma & Mathew, 1971; Dixit & Moorjain, 1981; Prayag & Nirmala, 1974; Rath, 1975; Reddy, 1978). On the contrary persons of poor and disadvantaged class show poor standing on all personality characteristics. These studies point out that social-classes vary in many ways-from highly advantageous to highly disadvantageous. They differ in economic condition, social status, cultural conditions, occupation, education, religion, dwellings (urban rural and jungle) etc. These variations cause differences in the personality characteristics of individuals.

But most of the studies taking personality characteristics have been conducted on general population (Non-tribal). There is lack of studies on tribal population. No doubt, important studies have been conducted in India and abroad on tribal population, but in most of these studies comparisons have been made between tribal and non-tribal groups (Chatterjee, 1975, 1981; Kumari, 1973; Paterson, 1962; Peck, 1967; Rokeach & Parker, 1970; Singer & Steffix, 1956; Singh, 1987). We still lack studies on tribal society alone. As the tribal society has under gone several social-cultural changes, it is therefore, important in this context to study the personality characteristic in relation to these social changes or variations in tribal society. The attempts of some investigator in this relation are worth mentioning. As for example,

Sarkar (1969) found differences in the super-ego pattern of tribal and non-tribals. Sarkar and Hassan (1977) also found difference in achievement motivation between the tribal and non-tribals. Balkrishna (1986) also observed differences in the cognitive and non-cognitive abilities of tribals and non-tribals. Bardiyar (1987) studies on Munda tribals and she found non-tribal higher on perceptual ability than the Munda tribal.

Thus the above mentioned and other related studies (Ziyauddin, 1985; Das Gupta, 1963; Bahadue, 1978; Ray, 1975; Saran, 1978; Shashi, 1978) show that there are several sub-groups in tribal society and they influence the personality growth and behaviour pattern of tribal people belonging to married social groups. Several studies have been conducted which show that values and interest of individuals are influenced by difference in social class situations (Taneja, 1969; Bhatt, 1966; Clair & Day, 1979; Nick, 1979; Feather, 1979; Sharma, 1976; Singh, 1986). It was expected, therefore, that tribals would also differ in their anxiety and adjustment with variations in social-classes which is more apparent in the case of the non-tribals and tribals. Non-tribals, are more in advantageous position educationally, economically and socially than the tribals. The tribals (aboriginals) are still living in their old totemistic life, following their old aboriginal practices and do not like to leave their rituals. But it does not mean that aboriginals have not been influenced by modern civilization. We see that industrialization, urbanization and statutory provisions by the Government have brought various changes in their jungle life. But the process of change is slow. Reports of the Parliamentary Committees constituted time and again to study the tribals of India are still a highly deprived class (Reports of the Advisory Committee on the revision list of SC & ST 1965; Reports of the working group to study the progress of SC & ST 1968; Census of India, 1971; & Census of India 1981).

Particularly the tribals of Chotanagpur have been highly exploited by the outsiders whom they call 'Diku'. The Mafiya, the money lenders, the contractors and other anti-social groups have virtually looted the poor and innocent tribals. The recent social tension, reflected in some of the tribal political organization 'Jharkhand Mukti Morcha', 'Jharkhand Sangram Samiti' etc., is the outburst of exploitations made to them. They are now becoming aware of these exploitation. Education, industrial growth, employment, opportunities and

The investigator visited the following schools for sample selection and data collection.

Rural area Institution

1. Maradits High School, Kuru
2. Kairo High School, Kairo
3. State Subsdised High School, Ghaghra
4. State Subsdised high School, Chandba
5. State Subsdised Higher Secondary School, Nadiya Lohardagga
6. Chunilal High School, Lohardagga
7. State Subsdised School, Gumla
8. Luthran High School, Gumla

Urban Area Institutions

1. St. John's High School, Ranchi
2. St. Paul High School, Ranchi
3. St. Analysis High School, Ranchi
4. Gouri Dutta Mandlia High School, Ranchi
5. Bal Krishna High School, Ranchi.
6. Zila High School, Ranchi.
7. St. Joseph's High School, Kanke.

Out of the students reading in matriculation classes in these schools only 638 tribal and 755 non-tribal students fulfilled the above mentioned criterion. With the help of Tippetts (1947) table of random numbers, 300 tribal and 300 non-tribal students were selected for the study.

Tests Used

Since the present research is designed to investigate into the anxiety, adjustment and fourteen dimensions of personality of tribal and non-tribal, rural and urban school students (the age group of 14 to 17 yrs.), the problem was to locate suitable and appropriate tests for the purpose.

Keeping in view the objective of the investigation the following tests were used-

1. Personal Data Sheet
2. Cattell's Fourteen P F Questionnaire-Indian adaptation by Kapoor and Mehrotra (1967)
3. Adjustment Inventory of Sinha and Singh (1984)
4. Anxiety Scale of Sinha (1968)

I. Personal Data Sheet (PDS)

A specially prepared data sheet was used in the study by the investigator. The PDS contained simple questions in Hindi to obtain information regarding the age, education, sex, residence and other personal characteristics of the subjects.

II. Cattell's Fourteen Personality Factors Questionnaire (HSPQ)

An Indian adaptation of the Cattell's fourteen PF in Hindi has been developed by Kapoor and Mehrotra (1967). This questionnaire which measures fourteen dimensions of personality was found useful for the present study. Besides, to suit the convenience of the Hindi speaking subjects of the sample its Hindi adaptation was available with norms drawn from Indian school students. The questionnaire has two forms namely A & B in which form A & B were parallel hence Form B was selected for the purpose. Junior (Jr.) Senior (Sr.) High School personality questionnaire invented by Cattell (1962, 1963) was designed to measure the fourteen dimensions of personality of ages 12 to 13 years school students. The items of this tests are related to the fourteen dimensions of personality and each dimension is measured by the HSPQ has a technical name, and an alphabetic symbol for purposes of rapid reference, e.g. ABC etc. Each dimension is defined by two poles (extremes). Each pole of the each factor describes the list of behaviours, presented to left and right of the extreme opposite characteristics.

However, it does not mean that the high score on the test having always to the right-hand-pole are necessarily "good" in some psychological sense and the low score to the left-hand-pole are "bad". In case of the measurement of personality, each type of temperature has usually both in good and its bad points. As for example, in dimension A, the

high scoring warmhearted person is rated as good natured, attentive to people, and trustful, but his enjoyingness means that his promises do not always mean as much as those of a person at the low-score pole. This is but one example, both good and bad are typically found at either pole on most of the HSPQ Personality factors (Cattell, 1962, 1963).

Table 2.1 : Titles and Symbols for Designating the Fourteen Dimensions

		Low Sten Score Description (1–3)	*Alphabetic Designation of Factor*	*High Sten Score Description (8–10)*	
Professional Term	(A–)	Sizothymia	A	Affectothymia	(A+)
Popular Terms		Reserved, detached critical, aloof, stiff		Warmhearted, outgoing, easygoing participating	
Professional	(B–)	Low intelligence (Crystallized, power measure)	B	High intelligence (Crystallized, power measure)	(B+)
Popular		Dull		Bright	
Professional	(C–)	Lower ego strength	C	Higher ego stre-	(C+)
Popular		Affected by feelings, emotionally less stable, easily upset, changeable		Emotionally stable, mature, faces reality calm	
Professional	(D–)	Phlegmatic temperament	D	Excitability	(D+)
Popular		Undemonstrative, deliberate, inactive, stodgy		Excitable, impatient, demanding, overactive, unrestrained	
Professional	(E–)	Submissiveness	E	Dominance	(E+)
Popular		Obedient, mild, easily led, docile, accommodating		Assertive, aggressive, stubborn	

(Contd...)

Table 2.1 : (contd.)

		Low Sten Score Description (1–3)	*Alphabetic Designation of Factor*	*High Sten Score Description (8–10)*	
Professional	(F–)	Desurgency	F	Surgency	(F+)
Popular		Sober, taciturn, serious		Enthusiastic, heedless, happy-go-lucky	
Professional	(G–)	Weaker superego strenght	G	Stronger superego	(G+)
Popular		Disregards rules, expedient		Conscientious, persistent, moralistic, staid	
Professional	(H–)	Threctia	H	Parmia	(H+)
Popular		Shy, timid, threat-sensitive		Adventurous, "thick-skinned," socially bold	
Professional	(I–)	Harria	I	Premsia	(I+)
Popular		Tough-minded, rejects illusions		Tender-minded, sensitive, dependent, over-protected	
Professional	(J–)	Zeppia	J	Coasthenia	(J+)
Popular		Zestful, liking group action		Circumspect individualism, reflective, internally restrained	
Professional	(O–)	Untroubled adequacy	O	Guilt proneness	(O+)
Popular		Self-assured, placid, secure, complacent, serene		Apprehensive, self-reproaching, insecure, worrying, troubled	

(Contd...)

Table 2.1 : (contd.)

		Low Sten Score Description (1–3)	*Alphabetic Designation of Factor*	*High Sten Score Description (8–10)*	
Professional	(Q_2–)	Group dependency	Q_2	Self-sufficiency	(Q_2+)
Popular		Sociably group dependent, a "joiner" and sound follower		Self-sufficient, resourceful, prefers own decisions	
Professional	(Q_3–)	Low self-sentiment integration	Q_3	High strength of self-sentiment	(Q_3+)
Popular		Uncontrolled, lax, follows own urges, careless of social rules		Controlled, exacting will power, socially precise, compulsive, following self-image	
Professional	(Q_4–)	Low ergic tension	Q_4	High ergic tension	(Q_4+)
Popular		Relaxed, tranquil, torpid, unfrustrated, composed		Tense, driven, overwrought, fretful	

Psychological Meaning of the Fourteen Traits

Only when the psychologist has experience and wisdom regarding the personality structures, he will find that he can make good predictions in a given educational or clinical situation. In terms of general behaviour, the psychological meanings of these source traits are set out here.

For factor A the term affectothymia meant emotional expressiveness, and Sizothymia (from the Latin for "flat") meant dry, and restrained expression. In popular term the affectothyme, meant warm-hearted, sociable, sentimental, easy going relaxation, and interest in people while the Schizothymia meant reserved, likes working alone, introspective, more uncompromising, inventive and more dependable in meeting promises and obligations.

The person who scores low sten (1 to 3) on this scale tends to be 'reversed', while the person who scores high (sten 8 to 10) on it tends to be 'outgoing'. The highest ranking (A +) occupations in A factor are teaching and salesmanship and the lowest (A-) are those of the house electrician and research physicist.

Factor B is to add personality informations in most school and clinic predictions by a good, brief, general ability measure. Hence, it discriminates between the low 'intelligent' and 'high intelligent' persons. 'Low intelligent' means concrete thinking, lower scholastic mental capacity mental defect, dull, whereas "high intelligent" means bright abstract thinking and having higher scholastic mental capacity. A person scoring low on factor B tends to be 'low intelligent' person. On the other side, the person who scores his on Factor B is regarded as 'Crystallized'.

Factor C is one of dynamic integration and maturity as opposed to general emotionality. The pattern has been shown to exist among normals as well as in groups of 'neuroticism', and in the latter has been called by Eysenck, "general neuroticism" Eysenck (1947). Ego strength is commonly regarded as a factor expressing the level of natural dynamic integration, emotional control, and stability. Some learning theorists consider the achievement of integrative learning would also describe this but the work of both Eysenck (1953) and Cattell (1957) shows that ego strength is not entirely dependent on learning in home or school. Factor C appears to the core also of what is viewed as capacity for frustration tolerance. The C-individual, as shown by the responses items tends to be easily annoyed by things and people, is dissatisfied with the world situations, immature, neurotically fatigued, psychosomatic disturbances, hysterical and obsessional behaviour.

This individual with marked ego weakness may fail in adjustment very badly if moved out of his home environment. On the other hand a person scoring high on the test is identified as 'emotionally stable' calm mature, realistic about life, possessing ego strength, and better able to maintain solid group morale.

The D+ individual reports that he is a restless sleeper, easily distracted from work by noise, is hurt and angry if not given important positions or whenever he is restrained or punished, and so on. Similarly, the high-D-scoring individual, though likable and affectionate in quieter moods, is apt to be regarded as a considerable nuisance in restrictive situation since he is so "impulsive". As Pierson (1964) has shown, delinquents tend to be high on D, though it turns out that if this is the prime cause of their being in trouble the outlook for recovery is good.

Factor E measures 'Humbleness versus Dominance' dimension of Personality. The factor of dominance in human beings and animals, has been investigated by Maslow (1954), Allport (1937), and other personality theorists. The mode of expression of this trait in girls appears to be somewhat different from that in boys, though not to the extent that it differs in women. In either sex high dominance lead to disobedience, headstrong, self-will, independence and creativity of mind, and sometimes anti-social behaviour. One who scores low (e–) on this test is called 'humble' and is described as mild, accommodating, submissive, giving way to others and docile. He is often dependent, confessing, anxious for obsessional correctness and self-sufficiency. On the other hand a person who score high (E+) on this factor is assertive, aggressive, independent, stubborn, dominant and self-assured. He tends to be hostile, authoritarian and one who disregards authority. From the ascendance submission studies with Allport's test, it is known that dominance tends to be positively correlated to some extend with social status and is somewhat higher in established leaders than in followers (Cattell & Stice, 1960).

Factor F measures 'Sober Versus happy-go-Lucky' Personality dimension. A person scoring low on the test is called 'Sober' he is considered to be prudent, serious, depressed, restrained, and introspective. He is sometimes pessimistic and unduly deliberate. On the other hand, 'happy-go 'lucky' is a person who scores high on the tests. He tends to be gay, enthusiastic, active, talkative, frank, carefree, expressive, quick and alert. He is frequently chosen as an elected leader.

On the whole, it would be seen that factor G best depicts the regard for moral standards, the tendency to drive the ego and to restrain the id, which are most frequently regarded as marks of the super-ego. This test measures 'Expedient versus conscientious' personality. An 'expedient' is a person who scores low on this test. He feels few obligations, tends to be unsteady in purpose evades rules and whose super-ego strength is weak. He is often casual and lacking in effort for group undertakings and cultural demands. His freedom from group influence may lead to anti-social acts but times makes him more effective, while his refusal to be bound by rules causes him to have less somatic upset from stress. On the other part, an individual scoring high on the test is called 'Conscientious'. He is preserving staid, and rule bound and painful. His super ego strength is stronger. He views himself as correct in, and a guardian of manners, and morals, preserving, painful, able to concentrate, cautious in thinking before he speaks.

Factor H measures 'shyness versus venturesome' dimension of personality. By 'Shy' is meant a person who is withdrawn, cautions, retiring, restrained etc. On the other hand, 'Venturesome' is a person who is socially bold, ready to try new things and spontaneous in expression and dealings. Low score on the test indicates a person to be shy. He usually has inferiority feelings. He tends to be slow and impeded in speech and in expressing himself. He dislikes occupations weeding personal contacts and prefers one or two close friends to large groups. On the other hand high scoring individuals on the test is called 'Venturesome' who is abundant in emotional response. His thick skinnedness enables him to face wear and tear in dealing with people and gruelling emotional situations without fatigue. He is generally careless about the details, and so he ignores danger signals, and consumes much time in talking. He tends to be pushy and actively interested in the opposite sex.

Factor I measures 'Tough minded versus Tender minded' personality. The person who scores low on this test is called 'tough minded'. Such a person is realistic, self-reliant, masculine, and independent. This type of person tends to be practical, responsible, but skeptical of subjective and cultural elaborations. He is sometimes unmoved, hard, cynical and smug. On the other hand, the person who scores high on this test is called 'tender minded'. A tender minded individual is dependent, over protected, sensitive, day-dreaming, artistic, fastidious, and feminine. He is sometimes demanding of attention and help, impatient and impractical. He dislikes crude people and rough occupations. He tends to slow up group performance and at times upset group morale by unrealistic business. Clinically this is an important factor, for neurotics are very significantly above normal upon it. Huffman's longitudinal study shows greater tendency, later to develop anxiety hysteria in those adults who were high Factor I as children. Although high Factor-I individuals behave as if they were insecure.

In questionnaire responses the J+ individual prefers to do things on his own, is physically and intellectually fastidious, thinks over his mistakes, and how to avoid them has private views differing from the group and avoid arguments. On the other part J-individual's activities are restrained to his group liking, attention-seeking and accepts common views and standards. This factor justifies more intensive research on its associations and origins.

Factor O measures 'Placid versus Apprehensive' personality. The person who scores low is a 'Placid' individual. A placid individual is described as self confident, expedient, cheerful, tough, does not care type, rudely vigorous and over confident of his own self and capacity to deal with things. He is resistant and secure. But when he feels the group is not going along with him he may evoke antipathies and distrust. On the counterpart a person who scores high on the test and is called 'apprehensive'. An 'apprehensive' individual is described as worrying, depressive, moody, full of foreboding and brooding. He has a children tendency to be anxious in difficulties. He feels over fatigued by exciting situations, and inadequate to meet the rough daily demands of life, is unable to sleep through worrying, is easily downhearted, and especially remorseful, feels that people are not as moral as they should be. In children, definite fears as well as a central feeling of inadequacy and loneliness are prominent for O+ scores, Cattell (1957). High scores on this factor is very common in clinical groups of all types.

Factor Q_2 is one of the major factors in the second order factor of introversion. This test measures "group dependency versus self-sufficiency" dimension of personality. The person who scores low on this test is called 'group dependent'. A group dependent individual tends to go along with the group and may be lacking in individual resolution. This type of personality needs group support and admiration. He prefers to work and make decisions with other people. On the other part, the person who scores high is called a 'self-sufficient' individual. A self-sufficient person prefers his own decisions. He is resourceful and temperamentally independent. He discounts public-opinion, but is not necessarily dominant in his relations with others.

He does not dislike people but simply does not need their agreement or support.

Factor Q_3 measures 'Undisciplined Versus Controlled' personality. A person who scores low on this test is called undisciplined'. He is self-conflicted, careless of protocol, follows own urges, not overly considerate, careful, or painstaking. He may feel maladjusted. On the other hand, the person who scores his on this test is called a 'controlled' type of person. Such an individual is socially precise, and following self image. He tends to have a strong control over his emotions and general behaviour. Effective leaders and some paranoids are generally high on this Q_3 factor.

Factor Q_4 measures 'Relaxed versus Tense personality. By 'relaxed' personality we mean unfrustrated, composed and satisfied individual. Conversely 'tense' personality is described as frustrated, excitable, restless and overwrought. The person who scores low on Factor-Q_4 is called 'relaxed' in some situations his over satisfaction leads to laziness and low performance. On the other part, the person who scores high tends to be 'tense'. He is often fatigued, but unable to remain inactive. In group he takes a poor view of the degree of unity, orderliness and leadership. Children and adults scoring high describe themselves as irrationally worried, tense irritable and in turmoil. The feel frustrated and are aware of being criticized by parents for phantasy and neglect of good goals.

It should be understood for statistical purposes that though the above 14 P.F. are distinct functional unities (so that each operates as a distinct pattern of behaviour), they will not as measurement, be entirely uncorrelated. There is unity of personality itself. Source traits are interrelated. For example, high intelligence, B, and dominance, E, and to be positively correlated, because success through intelligence tends to favour the development of confidence and dominance. Similarly, ego weakness, C-and ergic tension, Q_4, become positively correlated, because ego weakness reduces the possibilities of discharge of ergic tension. Of the fourteen scales of the questionnaire, all scales contain 8 times each, besides one initial item and one finishing items. For scoring, except test B, for all other tests maximum score of "two" is given. On test B every correct answer is scored one. Table 2.2. presents the number of items and range of possible scores on the different scales of the questionnaire.

Table 2.2 : Number of Items and Range of Possible Scores on 14 P.F. Questionnaire

S.No.	*Scale*	*Dimension*	*No. of Items*	*Range of Possible Scores*
1.	A	Reserved Vs. outgoing	8	9 to 16
2.	B	Less intelligent Vs. High Intelligent	8	0 to 8
3.	C	Emotionally less stable Vs more stable	8	0 to 16
4.	D	Stodgy Vs. Excitable	8	0 to 16
5.	E	Humble Vs. Assertive	8	0 to 16
6.	F	Sober Vs. Happy go lucky	8	0 to 16
7.	G	Expedient Vs. Consciencious	8	0 to 16
8.	H	Shy Vs. Venturesome	8	0 to 16
9.	I	Tough-minded Vs. Tender-minded	8	0 to 16
10.	O	Placid Vs. Apprehensive	8	0 to 16
11.	Q_4	Conservative Vs. Experimenting	8	0 to 16
12.	Q_2	Group dependent Vs. Self-sufficient	8	0 to 16
13.	Q_3	Undisciplined Vs. Controlled	8	0 to 16
14.	Q_4	Relaxed Vs. Tense	8	0 to 16

Reliability and Validity of the Test

Reliabilitiee: Consistency is, of course, the extent to which a test agrees with itself. The reliability form of consistency is the degree of agreement of a test with itself between two administration. The dependability coefficient (rd), is readministered after so brief a time interval that the trait itself is assumed not to have changed (by maturatism, learning, or fluctuatism).

Since the research undertaken on an Indian Sample, it was considered essential that the personality measuring device must be cross culturally valid. From this viewpoint Cattell's 14 P.F. questionnaire is a satisfactory instrument. Jahoda (1958) has shown that same fourteen to sixteen factor to exist in the Indian college students. Cattell (1957, 1962) reported that the 16 P.F. and HSPQ are now in use in twenty six different countries. For research has shown that these factors exists as patterns also in other cultures. The adapted 14 P.F. Questionnaire in Hindi; used in the present study, has also fairly high reliability on various indices. The details of reliability coefficients are given in Table 2.3.

Table 2.3 : Reliability Coefficients for the Fourteen HSPQ Factors Hindi Version

1. Stability Coefficients (Test Retest) : N = 2100

Factor	*A*	*B*	*C*	*D*	*E*	*F*	*G*	*H*	*I*	*J*	*O*	Q_2	Q_3	Q_4
Form A	.68	.61	.67	.59	.77	.67	.65	.65	.75	.51	.70	.70	.61	.77
Form B	.60	.55	.56	.58	.35	.56	.73	.56	.58	.46	.51	.57	.63	.62

2. Consistency (or Homogeneity or Split-half Coefficients) : N = 100
(Corrected to Full length by Spearman-Brown Formula)

Factor	*A*	*B*	*C*	*D*	*E*	*F*	*G*	*H*	*I*	*J*	*O*	Q_2	Q_3	Q_4
Form A	.79	.61	.80	.77	.52	.74	.82	.79	.73	.81	.86	.68	.93	.93
Form B	.81	.84	.87	.92	.60	.87	.89	.91	.91	.91	.92	.90	.90	.91

3. Equivalence (Parallel-Forms) Coefficients : N = 2100

Agreement between Form A & B	.49	.40	.52	.52.	31	.42	.51	.51	.40	.40	.71	.75	.75	.74	.76

So far as the validity of the Hindi adaptation of the test is concerned Kapoor & Mehrotra (1967) has provided evidence regarding the Direct Validities of the fourteen tests. The Validity Coefficients are given in Table 2.4.

Tabel 2.4 : Validity Coefficients of the 14 P.F. Questionnaire (Hindi Adaptation)

FACTORS SCALE VALIDITIES AS DIRECT VALIDITY

Concept validity coefficients (derived as the square root of equivalence)

Factor	*A*	*B*	*C*	*D*	*E*	*F*	*G*	*H*	*I*	*J*	*O*	Q_2	Q_3	Q_4
Coeffs.	.70	.63	.72	.72	.56	.65	.71	.71	.68	.84	.87	.87	.86	.87

Scoring of the Test

The completed answer sheet is the primary "record" from which the scores are obtained. All answer sheets scored by hand stencil key provided along with the test manual. The obtained scores on different factors which gave the raw scores were converted into stens, with the help of standardization table provided in the manual (Kapoor & Mehrotra, 1967) stens as in hand scoring, using two cardboard stencil keys, the raw scores for fourteen factors is obtained by simple digital weighting, which remains the best method for most users. For scoring, in all other tests, except test B, a score of two was given for every correct answer and for the incorrect one on test B every correct answer is scored 'one' and incorrect one as 'zero'.

Administration of the Test:

1. The HSPQ is planned for administration either in group situations, as in the classroom, or for individual testing, as in the clinic and in individual counselling, with equal appropriateness. In this group situations test, Form B was used.
2. A hand-scoreable answer sheet was used.
3. There was no time limit for the test. The average time needed to finish the form by high school student fall between 50 to 60 minutes.
4. Being answered that each students have the test booklet and answersheets, the researcher read the instructions given on the cover page on the inventory before the students. The students should also read the instructions silently along with the examiner.
5. It was to check time to time, that subjects were correctly matching test booklet and answersheets numbers.
6. The examiner should make every efforts to be the source of frank and sincere cooperation of the examinees.

III. Adjustment Inventory (By Sinha and Singh)

The Adjustment Inventory prepared and developed by Sinha and Singh (1984) in Hindi for use with Hindi knowing High School and college students of India, ranging in age from 14 years to 18 years. It is suitable for both the sexes. There are separate interpreting criterias for males and females. It has been designed to measure the adjustment level in the subjects. The tool is chiefly meant for discriminating well adjusted students from poorly adjusted ones of all grades in respect of three areas (Social, Emotional and Educational) of adjustment. The test is also useful in indicating the poorly adjusted students who may need further psychodiagnostic study and counselling. The Inventory consists of 60 items with forced choice response alternative of 'Yes' and 'No'. All the 60 items in the inventory covered the aforesaid three areas of adjustment.

To score a test record one mark is awarded for 'No' and 0 (Zero) for 'yes' response. The number of yes answers constitute the total scores and it yields the adjustment scores. The inventory is non-timed. In general, students take 10 to 15 minutes in going through the instructions and recording their responses.

Percentile norms were counted for both males and females of all the three areas (Emotional, Social and Educational) of adjustment separately as also for the whole inventory. Table 2.5 give the percentiles for males.

Table 2.5 : Percentile Norms for Males

Percentile	*Emotional*	*Social*	*Educational*	*Total*
P_{90}	9.98	9.88	9.95	26.89
P_{80}	9.10	9.16	9.11	23.41
P_{70}	8.11	8.24	8.34	21.34
P_{60}	7.21	7.38	7.40	19.36
P_{50}	6.18	6.58	6.48	17.74
P_{40}	5.91	6.00	5.98	16.06
P_{30}	4.42	4.91	4.82	14.32
P_{20}	3.11	3.75	3.33	11.77
P_{10}	2.01	2.70	2.02	8.82

The subjects can be classified into five categories in accordance with the raw scores obtained by them on the inventory. The five different categories of adjustment are, 'A' which stands for excellent, 'B' which stands for good, 'C' which stands for average, 'D' which stands for unsatisfactory, and 'E' which stands for very unsatisfactory adjustments. This categorization was done by dividing the base line of the normal curve into five equal units, each unit being equal to 1.2. Table 2.6 presents the classification of adjustment for total scores and Table 2.7 shows the classification in respect of the three areas: Emotional, Social and Educational.

Table 2.6 : Classification of Adjustment in Terms of Categories

Category	*Description*	*Range of Scores*	
		Male	*Female*
A	Excellent	5 & below	5 & below
B	Good	6 – 12	6 – 14
C	Average	13 – 21	15 – 22
D	Unsatisfactory	22 – 30	23 – 31
E	Very Unsatisfactory	31 and above	32 and above

Table 2.7 : Classification of Adjustment in Terms of Categories in the Three Areas

Area	*Category*	*Description*	*Range of Scores*	
			Male	*Female*
Emotional	A	Excellent	1 & below	1 & below
	B	Good	2 – 4	2 – 5
	C	Average	5 – 7	6 – 7
	D	Unsatisfactory	8 – 10	8 – 10
	E	Very Unsatisfactory	11 & above	11 & above
Social	A	Excellent	2 & below	2 & below
	B	Good	3 – 4	3 – 5
	C	Average	5 – 7	6 – 7
	D	Unsatisfactory	8 – 10	8 – 10
	E	Very Unsatisfactory	11 & above	11 & above
Educational	A	Excellent	2 & below	2 & below
	B	Good	3 – 4	3 – 4
	C	Average	5 – 7	5 – 7
	D	Unsatisfactory	8 – 10	8 – 11
	E	Very Unsatisfactory	11 & above	11 & above

Table 2.8 gives Means and Standard Deviations of the poulation upon which norms is based.

Table 2.8

Area	*Male*		*Female*	
	Mean	*S.D.*	*Mean*	*S.D.*
Emotional	5.62	3.12	6.55	2.81
Social	5.91	2.38	6.21	2.52
Educational	6.38	2.91	5.35	3.00
Total	17.91	7.36	18.11	7.27

Meaning of the symbols and explanation of the areas.

(i) Emotional Adjustment: High Scores indicate unstable emotion. Students with low scores tend to be emotionally stable

(ii) Social Adjustment: Individuals scoring high are submissive and retering. Low scores indicate aggressive behaviour.

(iii) Educational Adjustment; Individuals scoring high are poorly adjustment with their curricular and co-curricular programmes. persons with low scores are interested in school programmes.

Instructions for Test Users

1. It is a self-administering inventory. The examiner should read the instructions given on the front page and the examinees should also read them silently along with the examiner.
2. There is no time limit for answering it. Ordinarily an individual takes 10 minutes in completing the test.
3. Examiners should be instructed to interpret the meaning of the sentences themselves. However, meaning of the difficult words, if any should be given by the examiner.
4. Co-operation of the examinees is answering the inventory is very essential. The examiner should assure them that their answers and scores will be treated with strictest confidence.
5. The examiners should indicate frankly and honestly the purpose of the test, if and when any question regarding this is raised by

the examinees.

6. There is no need of telling why letters and numbers are placed before the questions. If, a question is asked about these the examiners should tell the meaning of the letters.

Reliability

So far the reliability of the test is concerned, coefficient of reliability was determined by (i) Split-half method (i) Test-retest method and (iii) K.R. formula-20 (0.95, 0.93 and 0.94 respectively).

Validity

In item-analysis validity coefficients are determined for each item by bi-serial correlation method and only such items were retained which yielded bi-serial correlation with both the criteria (i) total score and (ii) area score, significant level being .001 (Emotional X Social = .20, Emotional X Educational + .19, Social X Educational = .24).

IV. Anxiety Scale

This test has been developed by Sinha (1968) in Hindi, for Hindi speaking people-particularly the school and college students. It has 100 items which are to be annexed in Yes or No form. This test is applicable to the age-range from 14 to 18 years. It is applicable to both sexes (male and female) with different percentiles.

The scale can be regarded as an extremely popular measure of individual's manifest anxiety and his drive level. Low score i.e. below 25th percentile could regarded as indicative of poor motivation and sluggishness. Very high scores on it i.e. above the 75th percentile may be considered as symtomatic of such high state of anxiety which is likely to have disruptive and interfering influence on the performance of a complex task. The middle group of scores would represent essentially 'normal' individual with moderately good level to stimulate performance without itself providing as interferences (Sinha, 1968).

Items in the Sinha Anxiety Scale are classified into six areas of anxiety, viz., Health and appearance (HA), General Worries (w), Guilt and Shame (GS), Social Relations (SR), Psychological Symptoms (SPSY) and Physical Symptoms (SPH). Ten of them belong to the HA group, twenty four to W, eighteen to SR, ten to GS, twenty three to SPSY, and fifteen to SPH. Inter-correlation between six areas as also between each and total test score are high. A fairly high degree of generality between the areas is revealed.

Administration of the Test

It is a self-administering inventory. The examiner should read the instructions given on the cover page of the inventory before the examinees. The examinees should also read instructions silently along with the examiner.

1. There is no time limit for the test, ordinarily an examinee takes about thirty minutes times in completing the whole inventory.
2. The examinees should interpret the questions himself. The questions regarding the meaning or contents, should be answered by the examiner.
3. The examiner should make very effort to source the frank and sincere co-operation of the examinees. The examiner may assure the examinees that the results would always remain strictly confidential.
4. Questions from examinees concerning the purpose and use of the inventory should be answered frankly.

Scoring of the Test

The inventory can be scrod accurately by hand in three or four minutes of time. Each item which is checked as 'Yes' should be awarded the score of one. The score of every individual would be the total number of items checked positively. Higher scores indicate greater amount of anxiety in the subject.

Use of the Test

The present test is a measure of manifest anxiety and is useful for group administration. Like other tests of manifest anxiety this test can also be used in research, and survey purposes. With the help of this test one can screen easily high or low manifest anxiety score of subjects.

Norms

Percentile norms for the present inventory are given below. The subject can be classified into five categories on the basis of scores obtained on the inventory. The Table 2.9 gives the figure.

Table 2.9 : Percentile Equivalents of Tests Scores

Percentiles	*Boys Scores*	*Interpretation*
99	74	
95	60	Very high level anxiety
90	53	
80	44	
75(Q3)	41	High anxiety
70	39	
60	32	
50 Mdn	29	Normal range of anxiety
40	26	
30	23	Low anxiety
25 (Q1)	19	
20	17	
10	11	Very low level of anxiety
1	3	
N = 210	Mean = 31.46 Mediean = 29.40	SD = 14.90

Reliability

The coefficient of reliability was determined by split-half method and test-retest method.The test had high reliability both by the split-half and retest methods. Standard error of measurement was found to be 6.10, indicating that the true score did not deviate too greatly from their true value.

Table 2.10 : Reliability of Test

Method	*N*		*Index of Reliability*	*S.E.M.*
Split-half	239	.86	.92	6.10
Test-retest	88	.73	.85	

Validity

The validation criterion used for this test was to correlate the scores of that present test with scores of other valid test on manifest anxiety in Hindi. Its relationship with a very commonly used measure of anxiety viz. The Taylors Manifest Anxiety Scale (Taylor, 1953) has been determined in a study by Sinha (1961). It has been found that the anxiety level and its distribution are similar in the two sample of Indian and American college population. The test correlates 0.73 with the Taylor's Manifest Anxiety Scale. The high correlation between the two is indicative of the commonality of traits measured and of good validity. Hundal (1968) in his study of 200 male students of Punjab University has found score on the scale to correlate highly with those on other anxiety measures. Against Taylor's Scale, the correlation was .72 against Dutt's Anxiety Questionnaire (1964), it was .72 and against Cattell's Pat Anxiety questionnaire (1957), it was .70. Sinha (1965) claim that the test is a usual tool for assessing anxiety and it is efficacious in discriminating anxiety in normal and psychiatric cases. The high reliability and validity of the test and its standardization on an Indian Sample prove it as quite fair and highly suitable for use in India as measure of drive level and anxiety.

Procedure

For the present study the tests were administered to the two samples (tribal and non-tribal) in the following order:

1. Personal Data Sheet
2. Jr. Sr. HSPQ Form B
3. Adjustment Inventory
4. Anxiety Scale.

The procedure of data collection was apparently simple and straight forward. The researcher, first of all met the Head of every institution under study. Their cooperation, in fact was necessary, to get the required information about the students and collection of data later on. The researcher explained the importance of the study and assured that he would take the least possible time so that there is no disruption of regular routine and the teaching work of the school did not suffer. Thereupon, the investigator succeeded in getting the necessary permission and the class teacher was directed by the Principal to allow the investigator to collect the data. To these subjects the 14 P.F. Questionnaire of Cattell Jr. Sr. HSPQ Form B was administered then after their adjustment level and anxiety level were measured respectively.

Every subject was required to participate in the testing programme for two days i.e. taking personality test in one day and the other two tests i.e. adjustment Inventory and anxiety test were administered the next day. All the tests were administered in small groups of about 20 to 25 subjects each. Although no time limit was given for any of the tests in the present study, the subjects roughly took 10 to 15 minutes to complete the Personal Data sheet, 50 to 60 minutes for P.F. Questionnaire, 20 to 30 minutes for Adjustment Inventory and 20 to 30 minutes for Anxiety Scale. During the process of data collection, questions asked by the students were replied and classifications given and a good report was thus developed. It was observed that the subjects having been convinced of the importance and seriousness of the testing programme, gave their full cooperation to the investigator. Before leaving the institution the researcher thanked the students, their class teachers and the Headmaster. Thus the investigator succeeded in obtaining all the necessary data for the concerned research.

3
Personality Differences between Tribal and Non-Tribal School Students

Since the purpose of the study was to find out the difference between the two group-tribal and non-tribal school students in relation to HSPQ, Adjustment and Anxiety different subgroups were framed on the basis of the information collected by personal data sheet. In the present section, we are only concerned with whether the two groups (tribal-non-tribal school students) within different subgroups differed significantly with respect to HSPQ (Kapoor & Mehrotra, 1967), Adjustment (Sinha & Singh 1984), and Anxiety (Sinha, 1968). In order to analyse the data the *t* test used.

HSPQ

It was hypothesized that there will be significant difference in the personality dimensions of tribal and non-tribal students, as assessed by Cattell's HSPQ. Table 3.1 presents the summary of the results.

Results of *t* test on the HSPQ scores of tribal and non-tribal students in the various groups : Table 3.1.

1. On factors B,C,F,J,O, the tribal students differed significantly than the non-tribal students (t=2.01, 4.02, 3.05, 4.40, 5.97 respectively).
2. Tribal rural students and tribal urban students differed significantly on factors B, O Q_2, and Q_4 (t=7.27, 8.45, 2.22, 2.34, respectively).
3. There was significant difference between the non-tribal

Table 3.1 : HSPQ Scores of Different Sub-groups of Tribal and Non-tribal Students

HSPQ	Groups	T	NT	TR	TU	NTR	NTU	TU	NTU	TR	NTR	R	U
	N	300	300	150	150	150	150	150	150	150	150	300	300
1 (A)	M	4.85	4.86	4.99	4.72	5.25	4.48	4.72	4.48	4.99	5.25	5.12	4.6
	SD	1.43	1.69	1.48	1.38	1.71	1.58	1.38	1.58	1.48	1.71	1.60	1.49
	t	0.89		1.65		4.06**		1.39		1.42		4.14**	
2 (B)	M	4.26	4.50	3.65	4.88	4.85	4.16	4.88	4.16	3.65	4.85	4.25	4.52
	SD	1.58	1.31	1.33	1.58	1.29	1.24	1.58	1.24	1.33	1.29	1.44	1.47
	t	2.01*		7.27**		4.74**		4.39**		7.91**		2.23*	
3 (C)	M	1.80	5.36	4.83	4.79	5.83	4.89	4.77	4.89	4.83	5.83	5.33	4.83
	SD	1.27	1.47	1.31	1.22	1.44	1.35	1.22	1.35	1.31	1.44	1.46	1.29
	t	4.92**		0.43		5.81**		0.78		6.22**		4.43**	
4 (D)	M	5.76	5.71	5.65	5.88	5.61	5.82	5.88	5.82	5.65	5.61	5.63	5.85
	SD	1.49	1.47	1.55	1.42	1.46	1.48	1.42	1.48	1.55	1.46	1.51	1.45
	t	0.42		1.33		1.21		0.37		0.22		1.80	
5 (E)	M	5.21	5.32	5.27	5.14	5.88	4.77	5.14	4.77	5.27	5.88	5.58	4.95
	SD	1.36	1.63	1.44	1.27	1.55	1.51	1.27	1.51	1.44	1.55	1.53	1.41
	t	0.93		0.82		6.27**		2.32*		3.49**		5.16**	

Contd.

Table 3.1 : (Contd.)

HSPQ	*Groups*	*T*	*NT*	*TR*	*TU*	*NTR*	*NTU*	*TU*	*NTU*	*TR*	*NTR*	*R*	*U*
	N	300	300	150	150	150	150	150	150	150	150	300	300
	M	4.88	5.33	4.79	4.98	5.33	5.43	4.98	5.43	4.79	5.23	5.01	5.20
6 (F)	SD	2.03	1.47	2.51	1.37	1.38	1.55	1.37	1.55	2.51	1.38	2.04	1.48
	t	3.05**		0.79		1.21		2.67**		1.84		1.34	
	M	9.44	4.53	4.58	4.31	4.69	4.38	4.31	4.38	4.58	4.69	4.63	4.34
7 (G)	SD	1.43	1.54	1.38	1.47	1.58	1.47	1.47	1.47	1.38	1.58	1.48	1.47
	t	0.76		1.65		1.77		0.43		0.65		2.42*	
	M	4.53	4.63	4.61	4.45	4.74	4.53	4.45	4.53	4.61	4.74	4.67	4.49
8 (H)	SD	1.21	1.39	1.17	1.25	1.47	1.29	1.25	1.29	1.17	1.47	1.33	1.27
	t	0.98		1.18		1.31		0.56		0.82		1.76	
	M	5.69	5.47	5.70	5.68	5.46	5.49	5.18	5.49	5.70	5.46	5.58	5.58
9 (I)	SD	1.42	1.53	1.54	1.29	1.52	1.53	1.29	1.53	1.54	1.52	1.54	1.42
	t	1.76		0.12		0.15		1.15		1.33		0.02	
	M	5.22	5.71	5.15	5.29	5.58	5.84	5.29	5.84	5.15	5.58	5.36	5.57
10 (J)	SD	1.31	1.39	1.25	1.38	1.31	1.46	1.38	1.46	1.25	1.31	1.30	1.45
	t	1.40**		0.93		1.63		3.33**		2.90		1.80	

Contd.

Table 3.1 : (Contd.)

HSPQ	Groups	*T*	*NT*	*TR*	*TU*	*NTR*	*NTU*	*TU*	*NTU*	*TR*	*NTR*	*R*	*U*
	N	300	300	150	150	150	150	150	150	150	150	300	300
11 (O)	M	6.20	5.51	5.60	6.81	5.33	5.70	6.81	5.70	5.60	5.33	5.46	6.25
	SD	1.38	1.44	1.21	1.27	1.38	1.48	1.27	1.48	1.21	1.38	1.30	1.49
	t	5.97**		8.45**		2.20*		6.97**		1.77		6.89**	
12 (Q_2)	M	5.18	5.04	5.26	4.94	5.37	4.72	4.94	4.72	5.26	5.37	5.31	4.83
	SD	1.26	1.38	1.23	1.28	1.38	1.31	1.28	1.31	1.23	1.38	1.31	1.30
	t	0.49		2.22*		4.12**		1.42		0.70		4.52**	
13 (Q_3)	M	4.66	4.66	4.70	4.62	4.98	4.34	4.62	4.34	4.70	4.98	4.84	4.48
	SD	1.39	1.50	1.38	1.39	1.41	1.51	1.39	1.51	1.38	1.41	1.40	1.46
	t	0.01		0.45		3.79**		1.70		1.74		3.05**	
14 (Q_4)	M	5.98	5.98	6.18	5.78	5.98	5.98	5.78	5.98	6.18	5.98	6.08	5.88
	SD	1.51	1.44	1.44	1.55	1.35	1.52	1.55	1.52	1.44	1.35	1.40	1.54
	t	0.01		2.34*		0.01		1.16		1.25		1.67	

** Significant ∠.01   * Significant ∠.05

rurla and non-tribal urban students on factors A,B,C,D,Q_2 and Q_3 (t=4.06, 4.74, 5.81, 2.20, 4.12 and 3.79 respectively).

4. Tribal urban and non-trit al urban students were also differ significantly on factors B, E, F, J and O (t = 4.39, 2.32, 2.67, 3.33, 6.97 respectively).
5. A significant difference was found between tribal rural students and non-tribal rural students on factors B, C, E, and J (t=7.91, 6.22, 3.49, & 2.90 respectively).
6. On the whole rural students significantly differed on factors A, B, C, E, G, O, Q_2 and Q_3 (t=4.14, 2.23, 4.43, 5.16, 2.42, 6.89, 4.52. and 3.05 respectively).

From the perusal of Table 3.1 it is clear that the mean B (Dull-Bright) score of tribal student was 4.26 ± 1.58 as against the mean B Score 4.50 ± 1.31 of the non-tribal students. The difference between the two means (.24) was significant (t = 2.01, df = 299) beyond .05 level of confidence. The mean score of tribal rural students was 3.65 ± 1.33 as against the mean score 3.65 ± 4.88 of tribal urban student. The difference between the two means (1.23) was significant (t = 7.27; p = ∠.01). So far the non-tribal rural students are concerned, mean score 4.85 ± 1.29 as against the mean score 4.16 ± 1.24 of the non-tribal urban students. The difference between the two means (.69) was much more significant (t = 4.74, p = ∠.01). The mean score of Tribal urban students 4.88 ± 1.58 as against the mean score 4.16 ± 1.24 of non-tribal urban students. The difference (.72) was significant (t = 4.39, p = ∠.01). Again we see in the table that mean score of tribal rural students was 6.65 ± 1.33 as against the mean score 4.85 ± 1.29 of non-tribal rural students. The difference (1.20) was significant (t = 7.91, p = ∠.01).

Lastly, in general the mean scores of rural students on HSPQ is 4.25 ± 1.44 as against the mean HSPQ score 4.52 ± 1.47 of urban students. The difference (.27) was also significant (t = 2.23, p = ∠.05)

On factor A (Reserved-Warmhearted) only non-tribal rural students and all the rural students were significantly different as against the non-tribal urban stüdents and all the urban students respectively. The mean score of non-tribal rural students 5.25 ± 1.71 was as aginst the mean score 4.48 ± 1.58 of non-tribal urban students. The difference (.77) was significant (t = 4.06, p = ∠.01) Again the mean score of total rural students was 5.12 ± 1.60 as against the mean score 4.60 ± 1.49 of urban students. The difference (.52) was significant (t = 4.14, p = ∠.01).

On factor C (Emotionally less stable-emotionally stable) most of the groups differed significantly. The mean score of tribal students was 4.80 ± 1.27 as against the mean score 5.36 ± 1.47 of non-tribal students, the difference (.56) is significant (t = 4.92, p = ∠.01). Similarly, the mean score of non-tribal rural students was 5.83 ± 1.44 as comparison to the mean score 4.89 ± 1.35 of non-tribal urban students. The difference (.94) was significant (t 5.81, p = ∠.01). Tribal rural students were significantly differ (t = 6.22, p = ∠.01) from non-tribal rural students. The mean score of tribal rural students was 4.83 ± 1.31 as against the mean score 5.83 ± 1.44 of non-tribal rural students. On the whole the rural students were significantly differ (t = 4.43, p = ∠.01) from urban students. The mean score of rural students was 5.33 ± 1.46 as against the mean score 4.83 ± 1.29 of urban students.

On factor D (inactive - overactive) not a single group differed significantly (not significant even at .05 level). The mean score of all the groups was in average category.

On factor E (submissiveness-Dominance) only four groups differed significantly i.e. non-tribal rural and non-tribal urban, tribal urban and non-tribal urban, tribal rural and non-tribal rural and on the whole rural and urban students (t = 6.27, p = ∠.01; t = 2.32, p = ∠.05; t = 3.49, 5.16, p = ∠.01, respectively. Rest groups differed insignificantly (not significant even at .05 level).

On Factor F (Sober-happy-go-lucky) tribal and non-tribal students, tribal urban and non-tribal urban students differed significantly (t = 3.05, 2.67, p = ∠.01 respectively). The mean score of tribal students and tribal urban students were 4.88 ± 2.03, 4.98 ± 1.37 as against the mean score 5.33 ± 1.47, 5.43 ± 1.55 of non-tribal and non-tribal urban students respectively.

On factor G (Expedient - persistent) the mean score of rural students was 4.63 ± 1.48 as against the mean score 4.34 ± 1.47 of urban students. The difference between the two means (.29) was significant (t ± 2.42, p = ∠.05). Rest groups differed insignificantly (non-significant even at .05 level of confidence).

On Factor H (Shy-Adventurous) and I (Tough minded-Tender

minded) all the groups differed insignificantly.

On Factor J (liking group action-individualism) only three groups, tribal, non-tribal, tribal urban-non-tribal urban and tribal rural, non-tribal rural students was differed significantly. The mean score of tribal students 5.22 ± 1.32, tribal urban students was 5.29 ± 1.38, tribal rural students was 5.15 ± 1.25 as against the mean score 5.71 ± 1.39, 5.84 ± 1.46, 5.58 ± 1.31 of non-tribal, non-tribal urban and non-tribal rural students respectively. The mean difference was (.49, .55, .43 respectively) significant (t = 4.40, 3.33, 2.90, p = ∠.01 respectively).

On Factor O (Placid-Apprehensive) the mean score of tribal students was 6.20 ± 1.38, tribal rural students was 5.60 ± 1.21 non-tribal rural students was 5.33 ± 1.38, tribal urban students was 6.81 ± 1.27, and rural students was 5.46 ± 1.30 as against the mean score 5.51 ± 1.44 of non-tribal students, 6.81 ± 1.27 of tribal urban students, 5.70 ± 1.48 of non-tribal urban students and 6.25 ± 1.49 of urban students. The mean difference (.69, .21, .37, .11, .79 respectively) was significant (t = 5.97, p = ∠.01, t = 8.45, p = ∠.01; t = 2.20, p = ∠.05, t = 6.97, p = ∠.01; t 6.89, p = ∠.01 respectively).

On Factor Q_2 (Group dependency-Self sufficiency) the mean score of tribal rural students was 5.26 ± 1.23, non-tribal rural students was 5.37 ± 1.38 and rural students was 5.31 ± 1.31 as against the mean score 4.94 ± 1.28 of tribal urban students, 4.72 ± 1.31 of non-tribal urban students and 4.83 ± 1.30 of urban students. The mean difference (.32, .65, .48 respectively) was significant (t = 2.22, p = ∠.05, t = 4.12, 4.42, p = ∠.01 respectively).

On factor Q_3 (uncontrolled -controlled) only two groups i.e. non-tribal rural non-tribal urban group and rural-urban group differed significantly (t = 3.79, 3.05, p = ∠.01 respectively). The mean score of non-tribal rural students was 4.98 ± 1.41, as compared to the mean score 4.34 ± 1.51 of non-tribal urban students similarly the mean score of rural students was 4.84 ± 1.40 as against the mean score 4.48 ± 1.46 of urban students.

On Factor Q_4 (Relaxed-Tense) only one group i.e. tribal rural-tribal urban differed significantly (t = 2.34, p = ∠.05). The mean score of tribal rural was 6.18 ± 1.44 as against the mean score 5.78 ± 1.55 of tribal urban students. Rest groups did not differ significantly. They come in the average category.

Thus the perusal of the Table 3.1 we find no consistent results. Out of six *t* test on factor-A (Reserved-Warmhearted) only two groups differed significantly. On Factor-B (Dull-Bright) we find that all the groups differed significantly. So far the Factor-C (Emotionally less stable-Emotionally stable) is concerned only four groups differed significantly, and emotional stability come in favour of non-tribal, non-tribal rural and rural students.On factors D, H, I (Inactive-Overactive, Shy-Socially bold, Tough minded-Tender minded, respectively) all the groups differed insignificantly. The difference on Factor-E (Submissive-Dominance) only four groups differed significantly and shows that non-tribal rural, tribal rural and total rural students were more dominant in comparison to non-tribal urban, non-tribal rural and total urban students. Factor-F (Sober-Happy-go-lucky) indicates that only non-tribal and non-tribal urban students were happy-go-lucky persons. Similar is the case with Factor-G, (expedient-persistent, moralistic) and Factor-Q_4 (Relaxed-Tense) only one group i.e. tribal rural and altogether rural students were moralistic and fretful. On factor-J (Liking group action-individualism) only three groups differed significantly, which indicates that non-tribal, non-tribal rural and non-tribal urban students suffer with individualism. On Factor-O (Secure-Insecure) tribal, tribal urban, non-tribal urban and altogether rural students were significantly more insecure than non-tribal, tribal rural and non-tribal rural students. So is the case with Factor Q_2 (Sociably group dependent-Self-sufficient) and Factor Q_3 (uncontrolled-controlled) tribal rural, non-tribal rural and altogether rural students were significantly self-sufficient and controlled rather than urban students. Thus the result presents a differential picture of personality dimensions on different sub-groups. In this way we find that the results have by and large confirmed the conclusion drawn by Chopra (1967), Sharma and Mathew (1971), Dixit and Moorjain (1981), Prayag and Nirmala (1974), Rath (1975) and Reddy (1978) that persons of advantaged class possess more desirable characteristics. On the contrary persons of poor and disadvantaged class show poor standing on all personality characteristics. Tribal students come in the second category. Social class varies in many ways-advantaged and disadvantaged group. They differe economically, socially, culturality, educationally. They differ in their occupation, religion, residence etc. These variations cause differential effect in the personality characteristics of the individual. In the previous chapter we also saw that how child-rearing and modeling patterns influence the development of personality. There are three important methods of child-rearing practices adopted by parents— (i) democratic (ii) authoritarian and (iii) permissive. These three child-rearing methods have different effects on personality development. Social conditions vary in the technique of training and child rearing. Members of the upper class put high value on family status and past accomplishments and relatively low value on individual striving and aggressiveness, and so it is logical that they develop self-confidence, feeling of adequacy and even feeling of self-importance regardless of their own personal achievement. Further more, because of the more permissive child-training methods used in upper class homes, these characteristics are reinforced.

As we know that tribals are considered in disadvantaged group, they are deprived of so many facilities, which is availed by the upper caste. Since lower class parents tend to be inconsistent in child-training, swinging from extremes of permissiveness to extremes of authoritarianism accompanied at times by harsh punishment, their children develop feeling of inadequacy and loss of self-confidence, which increases with age. In addition, lower class children learn to be shy, secretive and dishonest in order to avoid punishment that inevitably follows non-conformity to parental wishes. Further, because of the lower class value emphasis on aggressiveness, especially for men, boys are encouraged to develop a "bully" personality pattern (Lipisitz, 1965), so is the case with present research. Thus the personality characteristics of an individual is influenced by the social class to which he belongs.

Adjustment (Social)

It was hypothesized that the tribal students will differ significantly as compared to the non-tribal students. The Adjustment Inventory for school students (Sinha & Singh, 1984) was used to identify social adjustment of the subject. Low score on social adjustment scale is indicative of aggressive behaviour. In order to verify the hypothesis the mean social adjustment scores of both the groups were calculated and *t*-test was applied to examine the significance of the difference between the two means. Table 3.2 presents the findings.

Table 3.2 : Comparison of Social Adjustment Scores of Tribal and Non-Tribal Students

G	*N*	*Mean*	*SD*	*t*	*df*	*P-value*
T	300	19.14	4.87	5.36	299	∠.01
NT	300	17.21	4.61			
TU	150	16.51	4.96	2.98	149	∠.01
TR	150	18.06	4.33			
NTU	150	16.01	5.31	3.52	149	∠.01
NTR	150	17.95	4.65			
TR	150	18.06	4.33	.22	149	N.S.
NTR	150	17.95	4.65			
TU	150	16.51	4.96	.68	149	N.S.
NTU	150	16.01	5.31			
U	300	16.26	4.98	4.83	299	∠.01
R	300	18.00	4.43			

Results of t test on the social adjustment scale of tribal and non-tribal students in various groups : Table 3.2.

1. The non-tribal students were less socially adjusted and more aggressive in comparison to the tribal students ($t = 5.36, p = \angle .01$).
2. Tribal urban students were significantly socially maladjusted than the tribal rural students ($t = 2.98, p = \angle .01$).
3. There were significant difference between the social adjustment of non-tribal urban and non-tribal rural students ($t = 3.52, p = \angle .01$).
4. There was no significant difference between mean scores of two groups (TR + NTR).
5. There was also no significant difference between the mean social adjustment score of tribal urban students and non-tribal urban students.
6. Over all rural students were significantly more adjusted than the urban students ($t = 4.83, p = \angle .01$).

The findings presented in Table 3.2 reveal that mean social adjustment score of tribal was 19.14 ± 4.87, tribal urban was 16.51 ± 4.96, non-tribal urban was 16.01 ± 5.31, tribal rural was 18.06 ± 4.33, tribal urban was 16.51 ± 4.96 and total urban students was 16.26 ± 4.98 as compared to the mean social adjustment score 17.21 ± 4.61 of non-tribal rural students, 18.06 ± 4.33 of tribal rural students 17.95 ± 4.65 of non-tribal rural students, 17.95 ± 4.65 non-tribal rural students, 16.01 ± 5.31 non-tribal urban students and 18.00 ± 4.43 rural students respectively. The difference between two means (1.93, 1.55, 1.74, 1.94) were statistically significant (*t* 5.36, 2.98, 3.52, 4.83, *p* = ∠.01 respectively).

The obtained result, however, is not in line with the finding of Bansal (1973) in which Hindu boys were reported to have significantly better social adjustment than the tribal boys. Though, illiterate, rustic and semicivilised, the community life of the tribals is well organised and may be called a model of corporate living. In the tribal life, the spirit of brother-hood has been responsible for the survival and integrity of the community. The tribals do not build houses for themselves away from others; they build villages and live together in harmony and peace. Their villages are not merely clusters of families living in physical proximity, but human habitations bound together by bounds of blood and commonality of interests. They are generally gentle and firmly believe in the principle of pacifism and social liberty. Unless disturbed or attacked they enjoy life and do not come in conflict with others. According to Kochar (1966) the Santals have a very high degree of social cohesion and social identity. All the social characteristics of tribals mentioned above go to explain the better social adjustment of the tribal students.

Adjustment (Emotional)

The hypothesis framed for verification was that the tribal students will differ significantly in respect of emotional adjustment as compared to the non-tribal students. As noted earlier Sinha and Singh's (1984) Adjustment Inventory for school students was used to assess emotional adjustment level in the subjects, on which low scores are considered as indicative of satisfactory adjustment. To compare tribal and non-tribal students in terms of emotional adjustment t test was computed. The results have been presented in Table 3.3.

Table 3.3 : Comparison of Emotional Adjustment Scores of Tribal and Non-tribal Students

G	*N*	*Mean*	*SD*	*t*	*df*	*P-value*
T	300	18.49	5.11	2.516	299	∠.05
NT	300	16.41	5.32			
TU	150	18.50	4.03	2.06	149	N.S.
TR	150	17.26	6.48			
NTU	150	19.14	4.87	5.49	149	∠.01
NTR	150	16.01	5.31			
TR	150	17.26	6.48	1.86	149	N.S.
NTR	150	16.01	5.31			
TU	150	18.50	4.03	1.28	149	N.S.
NTU	150	19.14	4.87			
U	300	18.82	4.50	2.77	299	∠.01
R	300	16.63	6.74			

Results of t-test on the Emotional Adjustment Scale of tribal and non-tribal students in the various groups : Table 3.3.

1. The tribal and non-tribal students were significantly different on emotional adjustment area (t = 2.51, p = ∠.05).
2. There was no significant difference between the group of urban tribal students and rural tribal students in terms of their emotional adjustment (t = 2.06, df = 149).
3. Non-tribal urban students significnatly differed from non-tribal rural students in terms of emotional adjustment (t = 5.49, p = ∠.01).
4. Tribal rural students were not significantly differ from non-tribal rural students on emotional adjustment (t = 1.86, df = 149).
5. There was no significant difference between the group of tribal urban students and non-tribal urban students in terms of emotional adjustment (t = 1.28, df = 149).
6. As a whole, urban students were emotionally less adjusted than

that of the counterpart of rural students ($t = 2.77, p = \angle.01$).

A perusal of Table 3.3 reveals that the tribal and non-tribal students differed significantly in terms of their emotional adjustment. The mean emotional adjustment score of the tribal students was 18.49 ± 5.11, non-tribal urban students was 19.14 ± 4.87 and total urban students was 18.82 ± 4.50 as compared to the mean emotional adjustment score 16.41 ± 5.32 of the non-tribal students, 16.01 ± 5.31 of the non-tribal rural students and 16.63 ± 6.74 of the total rural students respectively. The difference between the two means (2.08, 3.13, 2.19) were significant (t 2.51, $p = \angle.05$, $t = 5.49$, $p = \angle.01$, and $t = 2.77$, $p = \angle.01$ respectively).

It is also apparent from Table 3.3 that tribal urban students in comparison to tribal rural students, non-tribal rural students in comparison to non-tribal urban students and tribal urban students in comparison to non-tribal urban students had no significant difference. Thus the hypothesis that the tribal students will significantly differ in emotional adjustment as compared to the non-tribal students is partially confirmed.

Adjustment (Educational)

The next hypothesis was that the tribal students will differ significantly in educational adjustment as compared to the non-tribal students. The educational adjustment of the students was assessed by using the former inventory. In order to compare and show the difference between the group means t test was computed. The relevant data have been presented in Table 3.4.

Results of t-test on the Educational Adjustment scale of tribal and non-tribal students in the various groups : Table 3.4.

1. The non-tribal students were more adjusted on educational adjustment in comparison to tribal students ($t = 8.29, p = \angle.01$).
2. Tribal rural students were significantly more adjusted in educational area ($t = 9.29, p = \angle.01$).
3. Non-tribal urban students were educationally maladjusted in comparison to non-tribal rural students ($t = 8.36, p = \angle.01$).
4. Non-tribal rural students were better adjusted in emotioinal area as compared to the tribal rural students ($t = 2.30, p = \angle.05$).

Table 3.4 : Comparison of Educational Adjustment Scores of Tribal and Non-tribal Students

G	*N*	*Mean*	*SD*	*t*	*P-value*
T	300	16.31	5.74	8.29	∠.01
NT	300	12.41	6.13		
TU	150	15.51	6.08	9.29	∠.01
TR	150	10.12	4.01		
NTU	150	15.15	8.11	8.36	∠.01
NTR	150	9.13	3.81		
TR	150	10.12	4.01	2.30	∠.01
NTR	150	9.13	3.81		
TU	150	15.51	6.08	0.44	N.S.
NTU	150	15.15	8.11		
U	300	15.33	7.08	13.13	∠.01
R	300	9.62	4.11		

5. There was no significant difference between the mean score of tribal urban students and non-tribal urban students in the area of educational adjustment (t = .44).
6. On the whole, urban students were significantly maladjusted in educational area than that of rural students (t = 13.13, p = ∠.01).

The findings contained in Table 3.4 reveal that the tribal mean educational adjustment score 16.31 ± 5.74 was not better placed as compared to their non-tribal students having a mean score of 12.41 ± 6.13. The mean difference (3.90) was significant (t = 8.29, p = ∠.01). So far the tribal rural and urban students are concerned the mean score of tribal rural students was lesser (10.12 ± 4.01) than that of the counterpart of tribal urban students (15.51 ± 6.08). The mean difference (5.39) was significant (t = 9.29, p = ∠.01). Again it is obvious from Table 3.4 that there was significant difference (t = 8.36, p = ∠.01) between the mean educational adjustment score (15.15 ± 8.11) of non-tribal urban students and (9.13 ± 3.81) of non-tribal rural students. It is clear from Table 3.4 that there was significant difference (t = 2.30, *p* = ∠.05) between the mean educational adjustment score (10.12 ± 4.01) of tribal rural and non-tribal rural (9.13 ± 3.81) students. Table 3.4 also shows that the mean educational adjustment score of tribal urban students (15.51 ± 6.08) did not differ significantly (*t* = .44) as compared to the mean educational adjustment score of non-tribal urban students (15.15 ± 8.11). Lastly it is quite obvious in the Table 3.4 that mean educational adjustment score of urban students (15.53 ± 7.08) differed significantly (*t* ± 13.13, *p* = ∠.01) as compared to mean educational adjustment score of rural students (9.62 ± 4.11). In other words the rural students were more adjusted than the urban students in the area of educational adjustment.

Thus the expectation that the tribal students will significantly differ in the area of educational adjustment as compared to the non-tribal students is confirmed.

Earlier in the present investigation it has been shown that the tribal students have significantly more frequent and intense academic problems. Further there are studies (Srivastava, 1967; Das Gupta, 1963) which confirm that the tribal students have a number of problems in the academic sphere. Naturally, these problems will affect the educational adjustment of the tribal students. Thus it becomes apparent that the tribal students who have a number of frequent and intense educational problems are less educationally adjusted as compared to the non-tribal students.

Adjustment (Over all)

The last hypothesis framed for verification was that there will be significant difference between tribal and non-tribal students in overall adjustment. Adjustment was measured with the help of Adjustment Inventory (1984). The adjustment scores of the two groups were calculated and t-test was applied to examine if the two group means differed significantly. Table 3.5 presents summary of the results.

Results of *t* test on the Adjustment scores of tribal and non-tribal students in the various groups : Table 3.5.

1. The non-tribal students were significantly more adjusted than the tribal students (*t* = 16.02, *p* = ∠.01).
2. There was significant difference between the mean adjustment scores of tribal students and tribal rural students (*t* = 4.81, *p* = ∠.01).

Table 3.5 : Comparison of Emotional Adjustment Scores of Tribal and Non-tribal Students

G	*N*	*Mean*	*SD*	*t*	*df*	*P-value*
T	300	16.97	8.32	16.02	299	∠.01
NT	300	8.96	2.88			
TU	150	16.21	6.94	4.81	149	∠.01
TR	150	13.32	6.72			
NTU	150	9.82	4.45	10.39	149	∠.01
NTR	150	6.91	5.01			
TR	150	13.32	6.72	14.24	149	∠.01
NTR	150	6.91	5.01			
TU	150	16.21	6.94	14.86	149	∠.01
NTU	150	9.82	4.45			
U	300	13.01	4.31	7.07	299	∠.01
R	300	10.11	6.32			

3. The non-tribal rural students were significantly better adjusted than the non-tribal urban students (t = 10.39, p = ∠.01).
4. The tribal rural students were significantly less adjusted than that of non-tribal rural students (t = 14.24, p = ∠.01).
5. The non-tribal urban students were significantly better adjusted than that of the tribal urban students (t = 14.86, p = ∠.01).
6. On the whole rural students were significantly better adjusted than the urban students (t = 7.07, p = ∠.01).

Table 3.5 clearly shows that the mean adjustment scores (16.97 ± 8.32) of the tribal students was higher than that of the mean adjustment score (8.96 ± 2.88) of the non-tribal students. The difference between the two means (8.01) was also statistically significant (The t value being 16.02 as against 2.59 required to be significant at .01 level of confidence with 299 df). Thus it was confirmed that the tribal students were less adjusted as compared to the non-tribal students.

It is also clear from Table 3.5 that tribal rural students were more adjusted than the tribal urban students. The mean over all adjustment score of tribal urban students was 16.21 ± 6.94 as against the mean adjustment score 13.32 ± 6.72 of tribal rural students. The difference between the two means (2.89) was significant ($t = 4.81, p = \angle .01$). Again we see in Table 3.5 that non-tribal urban students were less adjusted than that of non-tribal rural students. The mean over all adjustment score of non-tribal urban students was 9.81 ± 4.45 as against the mean adjustment score 6.91 ± 5.01 of non-tribal rural students. The mean difference (2.91) was significant ($t = 10.39, p = \angle .01$). In comparison to tribal rural students and non-tribal rural students, there was also significant difference ($t = 14.24, p = \angle .01$). The mean over all adjustment score of tribal rural students was greater (13.32 ± 6.72) than that of mean over all adjustment score of non-tribal rural students (6.91 ± 5.01). So far the mean adjustment score 16.21 ± 6.94 and 9.82 ± 4.45 of tribal urban and non-tribal urban students is concerned respectively, there was also significant difference ($t = 14.86, p = \angle .01$).

Lastly it is also obvious from Table 3.5 that altogether rural students were more adjusted than that of the urban students. The mean over all adjustment score of urban students was 13.01 ± 4.31 as against the mean adjustment score of rural students i.e. 10.11 ± 6.32. The mean difference (2.90) was significant ($t = 7.07, p = \angle .01$).

The present finding supports an earlier finding of Bansal (1973) who has recorded that the Hindu boys have better adjustment than the tribals.

In explaining the results, it may be noted that despite marked and drastic social, political, economic and religious changes the tribal family is predominantly joint or extended. That the extensive social and geogrphical mobility appropriate to industrializing societies has negative consequences for extended kinship system is well known. It not only reduces the close ties between the adult generations and adult siblings but also generates conflict between the parental wishes and aspirations of the adolescents. More liberal views are held by these college educated boys concerning caste, race, religion, marriage, leisure time activities and so on. These views constantly conflict with the views of one or the other memebrs of the joint family. Besides city influences, industralization and assimilation of western ideas are affecting family togetherness. With educational opportunities for the tribal youths expanding in the cities, college going, youths are questioning the propriety of staying in a joint family which is not only ripped by family feuds and property divisions but also ceases to be an economically productive unit, especially in the urban setting. In a nuclear family the young tribals, who are better educated than their parents, can enjoy greater freedom than in past, parental authority loses its sting, mobility of self and children is facilitated and they can fulfil their economic aspirations easily. Also the joint family is now failing as a 'social security system' or 'emotional security system' for the young educated tribals. Besides the individualism fostered by modernisation tends to hinder the adjustment of the tribal students, thus the tribal family is in a flux and so is the adjustment of their young adults.

The finding can be explained in light of the fact in rural areas the family relationship is still very loving and a child gets plenty of affection from parents and other relations. In urban areas the family relationship is not so much loving because of father remaining mostly out of home and working mothers, in some case, do not devote that much time with the child as parents in rural areas afford to their children. Thus the adjustment of rural students (either tribal or non-tribal) are better as compared to urban students.

Thus the hypothesis that the adjustment of the tribal and non-tribal students will differ significantly is accepted.

Anxiety Scale

The sixth hypothesis was related to anxiety. It was hypthesized that there will be significant difference in anxiety score of the tribal and the non-tribal students. The results are given in Table 3.6.

Results of 't' test on the anxiety scores of tribal and non-tribal students in the various groups : Table 3.6.

1. There was significant difference in the mean anxiety scores of tribal and non-tribal students ($t = 2.38, p = \angle .05$).
2. There was no significant difference in the mean anxiety scores of Rural tribal students and Urban tribal students ($t = 0.33$).
3. The mean anxiety scores of non-tribal rural students was not significantly different from the mean anxiety scores of non-tribal urban students ($t = 1.57$).
4. There was significant difference in the mean anxiety scores of tribal and non-tribal urban students ($t = 2.30, p = \angle .05$).

Table 3.6 : Comparison of Emotional Adjustment Scores of Tribal and Non-tribal Students

G	*N*	*Mean*	*SD*	*t*	*df*	*P-value*
T	300	43.81	18.83	2.38	299	∠.05
NT	300	40.34	16.78			
TR	150	44.17	18.88	0.33	149	N.S.
TU	150	43.45	18.77			
NTR	150	41.86	17.49	1.57	149	N.S.
NTU	150	38.82	15.89			
TU	150	43.54	18.77	2.30	149	∠.05
NTU	150	38.82	15.89			
TR	150	44.17	18.88	1.10	149	N.S.
NTR	150	41.86	17.49			
R	300	43.01	18.24	1.28	299	N.S.
U	300	41.13	17.54			

5. The tribal and non-tribal rural students were not significantly different in their mean anxiety scores (t = 1.10).

6. Rural students were not significantly different from urban students on anxiety scores (t = 1.28).

Table 3.6 shows that the two groups—the tribal and non-tribal students differed significantly (t = 2.38, p = ∠.05) on the anxiety dimension. The mean anxiety score of tribal students was 43.81 ± 18.83 as against the mean anxiety score 40.34 ± 16.78 of the non-tribal students. The difference between the two means (1.05) was significant (t = 2.38) beyond .05 level of confidence. Table 3.6 also shows that the mean scores of tribal-rural did not differ significantly from the tribal-urban students. The mean anxiety score of tribal-rural students was 44.17 ± 18.88 as against the mean anxiety score 43.45 ± 18.77 of tribal-urban students. The difference between the two means (.72) was not significant (t-value .33). It is obvious from Table 3.6 that non-tribal rural students were not significantly different (the mean anxiety score 31.82 ± 15.89). The difference between the two means (3.04) was not significant (t = 1.57, df = 149) even at .05 level of confidence. Again we see in the Table 3.6 that mean score anxiety of tribal urban students (43.45 ± 18.77) differed significantly (t = 2.30, p = ∠.05) from the mean anxiety score (38.82 ± 15.89) of non-tribal urban students. Table 3.6 also shows that the mean anxiety score of tribal rural students (44.17 ± 18.88) was not significantly different (t = 1.10, df = 149) from the mean anxiety score of non-tribal rural students (41.86 ± 17.49).

Lastly it is quite obvious in Table 3.6 that rural students were not significantly different (t = 1.28, df = 299) from the urban students on their anxiety score. The mean anxiety score of rural students was greater (43.01 ± 18.24) than the mean anxiety score (41.13 ± 17.54) of urban students. Thus the present hypothesis is partly substantiated that the tribal and non-tribal students differ in anxiety. In other words tribal students were more anxious than the non-tribal students. This finding supports earlier finding of Sharaf and Singh (1977) who have recorded that the tribals are more anxious than non-tribals.

Social isolation is one important source of variance in anxiety. Schachter (1959) states that social isolation produces anxiety, and one of the consequences of experiencing an anxiety producing situation is a hightened tendency to seek affiliation relationships. Even after the impact of many forces the tribals are still socially isolated and facing a variety of socio-psychological problems. However, one may not deny the reality that the tribals are gradually abandoning their primitivity and are coming in contact with the people outside their community. No doubt education and political awareness are giving them a sense of identity with their fellow countrymen and are helping them in breaking their isolation, they still, however, feel themselves socially isolated which may be considered as one of the casual factors of higher anxiety level in them than non-tribals.

Further lower class children were found to be more anxious than middle class children by Dunn (1968), and Hawkes and Koff (1969). In addition Phillips et. al. (1969) found that lower class, Negro and Maxican-American children have higher anxiety scores even when the effects of defensiveness and other coping style variables were partialled out. Inspite of the best efforts by Government and non-Government agencies to raise the class level of Tribals, they are still treated as lower class people and they are even prohibited to eat and drink in the company of non-tribal section of the people. Thus it is natural that tribal, who belong to the lower class, are found to be more anxious than on-tribals. With specific reference to disadvantaged children, one of the critical findings is than the parents of such children communicate less openly that parents of middle class children (Maas, 1951). They also tend to have different approaches to discipline than their middle class counterparts, relying more on external control as opposed to casual thinking and internal control (Kohn, 1959; Kohn & Carroll, 1960). These aspects of lower class parent-child relationship cause difficulties when the child enters school, since communication and internal controls are highly valued in school. This may provide one casual factor in the development of anxiety in school. Tribals are socially disadvantaged, and the tribal parents also rely more on external control as opposed to casual thinking and internal control in disciplining their children. Consequently tribal students face difficulties when they enter educational institutions where communication and internal controls are highly valued. As such the tribal students may be expected to have more anxiety scores than non-tribal students.

Phillips, Martin and Meyers (1972) conclude that the higher anxiety of lower class and minority group children may be partly attributable to the primitivity or inadequacy of their defences and coping mechanisms. Tribal comes under lower class and minority group. The primitivity of the minority group of tribals is well known. Naturally they find themselves unable to utilize more adaptive defences to get rid of their anxiety as compared to the non-tribals.

Further, deficits in culture may also be one of the reasons in the development of anxiety in tribals. The tribals still adhere to the traditional culture. The tribal culture may be considered as an undeveloped culture. Traditional beliefs, norms and values have not yet been swept off completely and these guide the life of tribals to a greater extent. The tribals have numerous taboos and superstitions. For example, tribal-believes that spirits must be appeased and kept satisfied otherwise they may cause harm (Kochar, 1966). Most of their activities are centred around the achievement of this end and keeps them anxious.

4

Summary and Conclusion

The present research was undertaken to examine the differences between tribal and non-tribal students on fourteen personality factors (HSPQ-Kapoor & Mehrotra, 1967); Adjustment (Sinha & Sinha, 1984) and Anxiety (Sinha, 1968). On the basis of review of the studies the following hypotheses were formulated and tested:

1. There will be significant difference in the mean personality score of tribal and non-tribal students.
2. There will be significant difference in the mean social adjustment score of tribal and non-tribal students.
3. There will be significant difference in the mean emotional adjustment score of tribal and non-tribal students.
4. There will be significant difference in the mean educational adjustment score of tribal and non-tribal students.
5. There will be significant differnce in the mean over all adjustment scores of tribal and non-tribal students.
6. There will be significant difference in the mean anxiety score of tribal and non-tribal students.

The study was conducted on a sample of 300 male tribal and 300 male non-tribal school students. To have more clear results, the tribal and non-tribal students were subgrouped on the basis of their residence as rural and urban, and compared with each other. Thus altogether the groups are divided into six groups (T-NT, TR-TU, NTR-NTU, TU-NTU, TR-NTR, R-U). To examine the proposed differences between variables t test of mean differences were calculated. The following results were obtained as a result of the comparisons made on personality, adjustment and anxiety.

1. The tribal and non-tribal students differed significantly on some personality dimensions such as, Dull-Bright, Emotionally Less stable-Emotionally Stable, Sober-Happy-Go-Lucky, Liking group action-Individualism and Placid-Apprehensive.
2. Rural and urban students both tribal and non-tribal differed significantly on some personality dimensions (Reserve-warm hearted, Dull-Bright, Emotionally less stable-Emotionally stable, Submissive-dominance, Expedient-persistent, Placid-Apprehensive, Group dependency-self sufficiency, Uncontrolled-Controlled).
3. The non-tribal students were significantly more adjusted, emotionally and educationally than that of tribal students.
4. The non-tribal students were significantly socially maladjusted than that of tribal students.
5. Rural students were better adjusted in the area of social, emotional, educational and overall adjustment.
6. There was significant difference in the mean anxiety score of tribal and non-tribal students.

Thus the socio-cultural environment has deeper influence in shaping the personality structure of an individual. The groups are influenced to a great extent by the socio-cultural conditions he belongs. The studies conducted in this area reveal that individuals differ in their socio-cultural conditions ranging from extremely advantageous to extremely disadvantageous conditions. The studies also point out that advantageous and disadvantageous socio-cultural conditions cause the significant difference in the development of different components in the personality system of individuals.

In India castes, religions and tribes dominate the social scene. There are certain caste groups which have been socially and economically advantaged since a long past. But there are also some caste and tribes who have been in disadvantageous positions since time immemorial. Due to this differences, tribal students were attributed with undesirable traits of personality, they are more anxious and maladjusted.

In short the present study revealed the personality factors of the tribal and non-tribal students. It was found that the two groups differed significantly in relation to their personality factors, anxiety and adjustment.

Bibliography

Allport, G.W. (1937), "*Personality; A Psychological Interpretation*". Hennery Holt & Company. Inc. New York.

Allport, G.W. (1951). "*Personality*".

Allport, G.W. (1961). "*Pattern and Growth in Personality*". New York, Holt.

Bahadur, K.P. (1978). "*Caste, Tribes Culture of India*, Vol, IV, "Karnataka, Kerala and Tamil Nadu, ESS, Publication, New Delhi.

Balkrishna (1986). "Effects of Socio-Cultural Deprivations on some cognitive and Non-cognitive Abilities of Tribal Adolescents".

Baltes, P.B. and Nesselroads, J.R. (1972). "Cultural Change and adolescent personality development." *Develop. Psychol. 7*.

Bansal, J.P. (1973). "A study of the adjustment difference among the scheduled caste and high caste Hindu adolescene,t "*J. Edu. Psycho, Re. 1.*

Banseti-Fuchs, K.M., and Meadows, W.M. (1965). "Interest, Mental Health and attitudinal correlates of Academic Achievement among University Students." *British J. of Edu. Psychol.*

Bardiyar Parvati Kumari (1987). "A study of Cultural Impact on Research Indices Amongst the Munda Tribes of Chotanagpur."

Barton, K. (1971). "Block manipulation by children as a function of social reinforcement, anxiety, arousal and ability pattern." *Child Develop. 42.*

Beaglehole, Ernest (1949). "Cultural Complexity and Psychological Problems." In Patrick Mullahy, ed., A Study of Interpresonal Relations, New York; Hermitage House.

Bhat, C.L. (1966). "An Investigation into values of students at different age levels". Unpublished M. Ed. dissertation, Rajasthan University.

Biggs, J.B. (1959). "The teaching of mathematics II Attitudes to arithmetic - number anxiety." *Educ. Res.; 1.*

Blumberg, J.C. and Schmidt., H.E. (1970). "The relationship of academic performance of manifest anxiety in first year student teachers". *J Behavioural Sci.; 1.*

Boulding, K.E.et al. (1956). "The Image. "Ann Arbor: Univ. of Michigan Press.

Brar, J.S. (1970). "A study into the relationship of anxiety with academic achievement". *J. Educ. Psychol.*

Cattell, R.B. (1957). "Formula and table for obtaining validities and reliabilities of extended factor scales. "*Educ. Pscyhol. Measmt. 17.*

Cattel, R.B. (1962). "Handbook for the Junior-Senior high school personality questionnaire, "*Champaign Illinois* U.S.A. IPAT.

Cattell, R.B. (1963). "Early shool personality questionnaire." *Champign Illinois: U.S.A. IPAT.*

Cattell, R.B. & Stice, G.F. (1960). "The dimensions of groups and their relations to the behaviours of members." *Champign Illinois U.S.A. IPAT.*

Chatterji, N. (1975). "A comparison of Performance of Tribal and Non-tribal boys of Tripura on five performance Test". *MANAS* 22.

Chatterjea, R.G. & Paul, Bhaskar (1981). "Ecology field indpendence and geometrical figure recognition: A study in intelligence controlled condition. Personality Study & Group behaviour. *J. Abst. Vol. 1.*

Chopra, S.L:. (1967). " A comparative study of achieving and under achieving students of high intellectual ability." *Exceptional Children*, 33 (a).

Coleman, J.C. (1976). "Abnormal Pscyhology and Modern life".*G. Illinois*, England.

Cowen, H.L., Zax, M., Klein, R., Izzo, L.D., and Trost, M.A. (1965). "The relation of anxiety in school children to school record, achievement and behaviour measures". *Child Depelop,* 36.

Das Gupta, N.K. (1963). "Problems of Tribal Education and the Santhals." New Delhi Bhartiya Adimjati Sewak Sangh.

Devi, G.B. (1969). "A study of anxiety in mean and women college students." *Psychol. Stud.*, 14.

Dixit, R.C. and Moorjani, J.D. (1981). "Self concept and level of aspiration as related to socio-economic backwardness among young children." *Psycho-Lingna.* 11.

Dollard, Joh, Doob, Leonard, Miller, W., Neol, E. Mowrer, C.H., Sears, Robert R. (1961). "Frustration and agression". *New Haven, Conn, Yale Univer. Press.*

Draft Sixty-Five-Year Plan (1978). *Govt. of India Publication, New Delhi.*

Dubey, R.S. (1976). "Manifest anxiety, Sex differences and educational Performance." *Ind. Psychol. Rev.*: 13.

Dunn, J.A. (1968). "The approach avoidance model for the analysis of school anxiety. "*J. Educ., Psychol, 59.*

Dutt. N.K. 1964). "Psychological and Educational implications of the concept of mental health in Indian thought." Unpublished Ph.D. thesis, Punjab University, Chandigarh.

Eysenck, H.F. (1947). "*Dimensions of personality ability and Efficiency*" London, Kagan Pual Trench, Trubner and Co. Ltd., Broadway house.

Eysnck, H.J. (1953). *The structure of human Personality.* London Methuen.

Feather, N.T. (1979). "Accuracy of judgement of values system - A field study of own and atrributed value priorities in Paupa New Guinea", *International Journal of Psychology*, Vol. 14.

Feldhusen, J.F; Denny, T. and Condon, C.F. (1965). "Anxiety, influences of environment on the intelligence, school ahievement, and conduct of faster children"" in the Twenty-Seventh year book of the Nat, *Soc., Stud. Educ.* Nature and Nature, Part I, Their influence upon intelligence in Public School Publishing Co.

Freud, S. (1936)l. "*Inhibition, Symptoms and anxiety.*" London, Hogarth Press.

Frost, B.P. (1965). "Intellgience, manifest-anxiety and scholastic achievement." *Alberta J.Res.* 11.

Furneaux, W.D. (1957). "The selection of University Students." Report to imperical college of Science and Technology, London.

Gates, Jersild, T., Mc.Connell, T.R. Robert, Challman, C. (1971). *J.Educational Psychology.*

Gillian, J. (1955). "National and regional cultural values in the United States." *Soc. Forces.* 34.

Gokulnathan, P.P. 1971). "A study of achievement related motivation (n-achievement and anxiety) and educational achievement among higher secondary school pupils". *Ind. Psychol. Abstracts.*

Hallowell, A. Irving (1949). "The Social function of anxiety in Primitive Society,' In Haring, D.G. Personnal character and cultural Milieu, Syracuse Univ. Press, Syracuse. N.Y. rev. ed.

Hallowell, A. Irving. (1955). "*Culture and Experience*". University of Pennsylvania Press.

Harris, D.B. (1958). "Parental judgement of responsibility in children and children's adjustment".

Kawkes, T. and Kof, R. (1969). "Social class differences in anxiety of elementary school children". Paper Presented at AERA.

Hawkes, T.H. and Furst, N.F. (1971). "Race, Socio-economic situation, achivement, IQ, and teacher rating of student's behaviour and factors relating to anxiety in upper elementary school children". *Social. Educ.*, 44.

Hazri, A. and Thakur, G.P. (1970). "The relationship between manifest anxiety and intelligence". *J. Educ. Psychol*: 20.

Hodapp, V. (1978). "Anxiety during the period of adolescence". Fernsehen Und Bildung, Vol. 12.

Hundal, P.S. (1968). "Factorial Structure of Psychometric measurs of anxiety and academic achievement". Unpublished report.

Jahoda, M. (1958). "Current concepts of positive Mental Health". New York; *Basic Books.*

Joshi, M.C. and Tewari, J. (1977). "Personality development of children in relation to child rearing practices among socio-econmic classes." *Indian Psychological Review*, 4.

Keller, S. (1961). "The Social World of Urban Slum child". *Amer. J. Ortho-Psychiatry*, Vol.33.

Keller, E.D. and Rowley, V.N. (1964). "The relations among anxiety intelligence and scholastic achievement in junior high school children". *J. Educ. Res.* 58.

Kisker, G.W. (1972). "*The Disorganized personality*". Tokyo: McGrawHill Kogakusha Ltd.

Kluckohn, C. and Muray H.A. (1953). "*Personality in Nature, Society and Culture*". Alfred. A. Knopf New York.

Kochar, V.K. (1966). "Village deities of the Santals and associated rituals". *Anthropos*, 61.

Kohn, M. (1959). "Social class and the exercise of parental authority". *Amer. Social. Rev: 24.*

Kohn, M. & Carall, E. (1960). "Social class and the allocation of Parental responsibilities." *Sociometry*, 23.

Krabt, a. (1969). "A class for academic underchievers in high school." *Adolescence*, 4.

Krishna, K.P. (1971). "Manifest anxiety as a function of Sex and education". *Behaviroestic*, 1.

Krishna, K.P. and and Kumar, S. (1979). *Indian J. of clinic Psychol., Vol. 6.*

Kulshrestha, S.P. (1968), "Values and vocational interest of Intermediate Student", M.Ed. Diss., Agra University.

Kumari Gupta, Lata (1973), "A study of personality variables and attitudes and students in public schools, convents Sanik schools and Government Aided insitutions of Uttar Pradesh". Unpublished Ph.D. Thesis, Agra University.

Linton, B. (1945). "*The cultural background of personality*". D. Applton Century, Company, Inc. New York.

Lipistiz, L. (1965). "Working-class authoritarianism. A re-evaluation". *Amer. Social. Rev.* 30.

Lott. B.F. and Lott. A.J. (1968). "the relation of manifest anxiety in children to learning task performance and other variables". *Child Develop*, 39.

Ludin, R.W. and Sawyer,C.R. (1965). "The relationship between test anxiety, drinking patterns and scholastic achievement in a group of undergraduate college men." *J. Gen. Psychol.*, 73.

Lunneborg, P.W. (1964). "Relations among social desirability, achievement and anxiety measures in children". *Child Developm.*, 35.

Maas, H. (1951). "Some special class differences in the family systems and group relations of Pre-and early adolscents". *Child Developm.*, 22.

Mandelbaum, David, G./ (ed.), (1949). "Selected writings of Edward Sapie, Berkeley' Univ. of California Press.

Maslow, A.H. (1954)."*Motivation and Personality*". New York; Harper Bros.

Mattason, K.D. (1974). *J. of Educ. Psychol.* Published by American Psychological Association.

Mead, Margaret (1947). "The Implications of Culture change for Personality development." *American J. of Ortho-Psychiatry*, Vol. 17.

Merryman, E.P. (1974). "The effects of maniest anxiety on the reading achievement of fifth grade students". *J. Exp. Educ. Psychol*, 42.

Meyer, W.J. and Raymond,H. (1962). "Questionnaire-anxiety and Social Comformity,." *Psychol. Rep.*

Miller, H.,C. et al (1966). "Parental and environmental factor in late neurogenic sequelac." *American J. Dis. Children*, 112.

Montagu, A. (1962). "*Parental influence*". Spring field III, Charles, C. Thomas.

Moore, R.Y. (1962). *Psychological Abstracts.* Vol. 36.

Moore, R.Y. (1965). "*Sub-Cortical mechanisms of behaviour.*" New York; Basic Books Inc.

Table 2.1 : (contd.)

		Low Sten Score Description (1–3)	*Alphabetic Designation of Factor*	*High Sten Score Description (8–10)*	
Professional	(Q_2-)	Group dependency	Q_2	Self-sufficiency	(Q_2+)
Popular		Sociably group dependent, a "joiner" and sound follower		Self-sufficient, resourceful, prefers own decisions	
Professional	(Q_3-)	Low self-sentiment integration	Q_3	High strength of self-sentiment	(Q_3+)
Popular		Uncontrolled, lax, follows own urges, careless of social rules		Controlled, exacting will power, socially precise, compulsive, following self-image	
Professional	(Q_4-)	Low ergic tension	Q_4	High ergic tension	(Q_4+)
Popular		Relaxed, tranquil, torpid, unfrustrated, composed		Tense, driven, overwrought, fretful	

Psychological Meaning of the Fourteen Traits

Only when the psychologist has experience and wisdom regarding the personality structures, he will find that he can make good predictions in a given educational or clinical situation. In terms of general behaviour, the psychological meanings of these source traits are set out here.

For factor A the term affectothymia meant emotional expressiveness, and Sizothymia (from the Latin for "flat") meant dry, and restrained expression. In popular term the affectothyme, meant warm-hearted, sociable, sentimental, easy going relaxation, and interest in people while the Schizothymia meant reserved, likes working alone, introspective, more uncompromising, inventive and more dependable

in meeting promises and obligations.

The person who scores low sten (1 to 3) on this scale tends to be 'reversed', while the person who scores high (sten 8 to 10) on it tends to be 'outgoing'. The highest ranking (A +) occupations in A factor are teaching and salesmanship and the lowest (A-) are those of the house electrician and research physicist.

Factor B is to add personality informations in most school and clinic predictions by a good, brief, general ability measure. Hence, it discriminates between the low 'intelligent' and 'high intelligent' persons. 'Low intelligent' means concrete thinking, lower scholastic mental capacity mental defect, dull, whereas "high intelligent" means bright abstract thinking and having higher scholastic mental capacity. A person scoring low on factor B tends to be 'low intelligent' person. On the other side, the person who scores his on Factor B is regarded as 'Crystallized'.

Factor C is one of dynamic integration and maturity as opposed to general emotionality. The pattern has been shown to exist among normals as well as in groups of 'neuroticism', and in the latter has been called by Eysenck, "general neuroticism" Eysenck (1947). Ego strength is commonly regarded as a factor expressing the level of natural dynamic integration, emotional control, and stability. Some learning theorists consider the achievement of integrative learning would also describe this but the work of both Eysenck (1953) and Cattell (1957) shows that ego strength is not entirely dependent on learning in home or school. Factor C appears to the core also of what is viewed as capacity for frustration tolerance. The C-individual, as shown by the responses items tends to be easily annoyed by things and people, is dissatisfied with the world situations, immature, neurotically fatigued, psychosomatic disturbances, hysterical and obsessional behaviour.

This individual with marked ego weakness may fail in adjustment very badly if moved out of his home environment. On the other hand a person scoring high on the test is identified as 'emotionally stable' calm mature, realistic about life, possessing ego strength, and better able to maintain solid group morale.

The D+ individual reports that he is a restless sleeper, easily distracted from work by noise, is hurt and angry if not given important positions or whenever he is restrained or punished, and so on. Similarly,

Journal of Indian Socio-Psycho. Studies P.G. Deptt. of Psychology, Ranchi University.

Sarsenrath, J.M. (1967). "Anxiety, aptitude, attitude and achievement". *Psychology in Schools*, 4.

Satyarthi, M.K. (1977). "*Anxious attitude of students in relation to some background variables.*" 64th session of Indn. Sc. Cong.

Saul, L.J. et al. (1937). "Correlations between electro encephalograms and psychological orgnisation of the individual." *Trans. Amer. Neurol. Assoc.* Vol. 63.

Saxena, A.K. et al. (1981). *Indian Psychological Review*. Vol. 20 (4).

Saxena, P. (1965). "Anxiety and its effects on adolescent achievement." *Res. J. Philosophy and Soc. Sci.* 2.

Schachter, S. (1959). *"The Psychology of Affiliation."* Palo Alto, Calfornia: Sanford Univ. Press.

Schuasaler, K.F. and Cressey, D.R. (1950). Personality characteristics of criminals." *Amer. J. of Soc.* 5.

Shanker, U. and Brar. J.S. (1973). "A study into the relationship of anxiety with academic achievement." *J. Educ. Psychol.* 30.

Sharaft, H. and Singh, A.K. (1977). "Social disadvantages attitudes and Personality." Cyclostyled P.G. Deptt. of Psychology, Ranchi University.

Sharma, S. (1970). "Manifest anxiety and school achievement of adolscents." *J. Consult. Clin. Psychol.* 34.

Sharma, S. (1976). "Some Personality characteristics of Female College students of different socio-economic backgrounds". Unpublished Ph.D.Thesis of Patna University.

Sharma, V.P. and Mathew, M.A. (1971). "The relationship of aspiration to intelligence and scholastic achievement of deprived and privileged pupils." *Behaviouristic*. Vol. 1(1).

Shashi, S.S. (1978). "*Night life of Indian Tribes.*" Agam Prakashan, Delhi.

Singer, S.L. and Steffix, B. (1956). "Sex differences in job values and Desires." *J. Soc. Psychol.* 43.

Singh, A. (1981). "The effect of School environment on Personality and ability structure." *Personality study & group Behaviour*. Vol. 1(1).

Singh, A.J. (1971). "A study of relationship between anxiety and academic achievement of University Students." *New Trends in Education*, 2.

Singh, B.& Kumar, P. (1977). "Anxiety and educational achievement." *J. of Psychological Researches*. Vol. 21 (1).

Singh, C.M. (1989). "An Impirical study of value system and interest Pattern of Tribal Students." Unpub. Ph.D. Thesis of Magadh Univ. of Both Gaya.

Singh, L.B. (1978). "Are high rigid individuals more anxiour ? "*Indian J. of Clinc. Psychol.* Vol. 5(1).

Singh, M. (1986). "Interest and values of Advantaged and disadvantaged groups of college students."

Singh, S. (1987). "Interest values and problems of the Tribal students of Bihar," Magadh University, Ph.D. Dissertation. Both Gaya.

Singh, S.B. and Nigam, A. (1973). "A comparative study of personality Profile of the male and female medical students." *Indian J. Psychomet. Educ.* 4.

Singh, S.D. et al. (1977). "Anxiety pattern among adolscent." Manas Vol. 24 (1).

Singh, V. (1976). "Determinants of choice of students of University level", *J. of higher education*, 2 No. 2.

Singhal, W.R. (1974). 'A study of relationship between anxiety and academic achievement." *J. Educ. Res. Exten.*

Sinha, A.K.P. and Singh, R.P. (1984). Mannual for adjustment inventory for school students. National Psychological Corporation, Agra.

Sinha, D. (1961). "*Development of two anxiety scales.* "Manas.

Sinha, D. (1965). "An analysis of anxiety areas and manifestations: a factorial study. "*J. Psychol. Res.* 9.

Sinha, D. (1966). "A Psychological analysis of some factors associated with success and failure in university education; a summary of

findings." *Ind. Educ., Res.* 1.

Sinha, D (1968). "Mannual for Sinha W-A. Self-analysis Form (anxiety-scale)." Rupa Psychological Corporation, Varanasi.

Sinha, D. et al. (1970). "*Academic achievers and Achievers.* "United Publishers Allahabad.

Sinha, N.C.P. (1972). "*Intelligence and Scholastic achievement.*Manas, 19.

Sontag, L. W. (1966). "Implication of fetal behaviour for adult personalities, "*Ann. N.Y. Acad. Sci.* 132.

Spiro, M.e., (1951). "Culture and Personality." The Natural History of a False Dichotomy. *Psychiatry*, 14.

St. Clair, S. and Day, H.D. (1979). *J. of Youth and Adolscent*, Vol. 8(3).

Stevenson, H.W. and Iscoe, 1 (1956). "Anxeity and discrimation learning." *Amer. J. Psychol.* 69.

Taneja, N. (1969). "A comparative study of values among adolescent boys and girls." Unpublished M.Ed. Dissertation, Deptt. of Education, Kurukshetra University.

Taylor, J.A. (1953). "Personality scale of manifest anxiety." *J. Abnormal. Soc. Psychol.* 48.

Terman, L.M. and Taylor, L.E. (1954). "Psychological Sex differences in L. Carmichall (ed.)", *Mannual of child Psychology.* New York, Wiley.

Tripathy, S.N. (1969). "Creativity and Education, Regional College of Education".

Vaugham, G. and Taylor, A.J. (1966). "Clininal anxiety and conformity." *Percept. Mot. Skills.*, 22.

Vidyarthi, L.P. (1964). "*Cultural Contours of Tribal Bihar,*" Puntho Pustak, Calcutta.

Wallac, Anthony, F.C. (1961). "The Psychic Unity of Human Groups." In Bert Kaplan ed, studying personality cross-culturally. Evanston: Row, Peterson.

Wallac, Anthony, F.C. and Atkins, Joh, (1960). :The Meaning of Kinship Terms." *American Anthropologist.* 62.

White, Leslie (1959). "The concept of culture." *American Anthropoligist.* 61.

Ziyauddin, A. (1985). "*Bihar Ke Adibasi.*" Delhi Motilal Banarsi Das.

Index